The Jericho Plan
Breaking Down the Walls
Which Prevent
Post-Abortion Healing

David C. Reardon, Ph.D.

Acorn Books
Springfield, Illinois

Dedicated to my parents, Tom and Joan,
who offered their children examples of faith, hope, and charity

The Jericho Plan: Breaking Down the Walls Which Prevent Post-Abortion Healing,
Copyright © 1996 David C. Reardon, Ph.D.

Published by Acorn Books, P.O. Box 7348, Springfield, IL 62791-7348.

Cover painting: "Her Choice," original oil on linen, 16"× 20", ©1996 by Diana Moses Botkin,
used with permission

Cover and text design: C. J. Petlick, Hunter Design Associates

Printed in Canada

Portions of this book have been adapted from these previous works by the author:
    David C. Reardon, *Making Abortion Rare: A Healing Strategy for a Divided Nation*
        (Springfield, IL: Acorn Books, 1996).
    "A Healing Strategy" *The Post-Abortion Review* 3(1):1-4 (1995).
    "Despair Versus Hope" *The Post-Abortion Review* 3(2):1-2 (1995).

Cataloging-in-Publication Data
Reardon, David C., Ph.D.
    The jericho plan:breaking down the walls which prevent post-abortion healing /
David C. Reardon
    p.   cm.
    Bibliography: (p.   )
    Includes bibliographical references.
    ISBN 0-9648957-5-7 (paper)
    1. Abortion counseling.
    2. Abortion applicants—Pastoral counseling of.
    3. Abortion—United States—Psychological aspects.
    4. Abortion—Religious aspects—Christianity.
    5. Abortion—Moral and ethical aspects.
    I. Title.
    HQ767.4   1996   363.4'6   LCCN: 95-83667
                                                     CIP

**Attention Non-Profit Organizations, Colleges, Universities, and Professional
Organizations:** Quantity discounts are available on bulk purchases of this book for
educational training, fund raising, or gift giving. Special books, booklets, or book
excerpts can also be prepared to fit your specific needs. For information contact:
Marketing Department, Acorn Books, PO Box 7348, Springfield, IL 62791-7348.

CONTENTS

WHO SHOULD USE THIS BOOK?

Our goal, in this book, is to promote the emotional and spiritual healing of women and men who have been scarred by abortion. While this text is specifically directed toward clergy, there is no reason for this message of hope to be confined strictly to the pulpit. Indeed, one of our requests of clergy is that they seek to make all members of their congregations ambassadors of God's healing love.

Therefore, if you are a person who simply knows someone who has had an abortion (and we all do know such people, even if their abortions have been kept a secret from us), you will benefit from this book. You will be better prepared to offer the words of understanding and healing which are so desperately needed by the post-aborted women and men whose lives you touch. While you will probably never be in a position to give a sermon on this topic, you have the equally important task of being an ambassador of God's mercy in your daily, one-on-one contacts. This book will free you from the fear of "saying the wrong thing."

If you yourself have been involved in an abortion, this book will address many of the concerns and questions which you still have. Of special importance are its answers to the troubling questions that are most *difficult* for you to ask. It will also help you to see that you are not alone. Others have experienced and overcome the same problems. Their insights can help you to better understand what you have been through, why you continue to struggle, and how you can finally find peace of mind and heart. Indeed, when you complete the journey upon which you are embarking, you may well discover a greater joy of spirit than you have ever known. We encourage you to draw upon the resources at the end of this book, especially for the purpose of contacting others who have been down this same path of healing. Because of their first-hand experience, they can make your journey much easier.

So, this book is really for everyone who cares about the people whose lives have been touched by abortion. While we encourage you to buy copies for friends and loved ones who have been involved in abortions, plus all the clergy in your area (which is why we have a generous discount for bulk orders), don't become a distributor until you read it yourself. To simply provide helpful information to others is a good, but rather mundane task. Our hope is that *you* will become a healer, a witness to God's unfathomable mercy.

Our world most desperately needs healers. Do not be timid. Be a healer.

Introduction

No one enjoys preaching about abortion. Most of us would rather avoid it, because we know the abortion issue touches a deeply personal and painful memory for so many people in our congregations. But avoiding the abortion issue does not help anyone. People on both sides of the issue need to look more deeply at the abortion issue in a way they have never done before.

Pro-life members need to learn greater compassion and understanding about why women have abortions, and what they go through afterward. Heaping shame and scorn on those who have had abortions is counterproductive. It creates resentment and drives away those who most desperately need assurance of God's healing love.

At the same time, those who have been involved in abortion need to feel understood. They need help to see how they can break through the walls abortion has created in their lives. They need to hear God's word directly addressed to their own experience with abortion so that they can turn with confidence to the hope of being fully reconciled with Christ.

Finally, abortion defenders (who have not personally experienced the reality of abortion) need to learn that abortion is not a panacea for problem pregnancies. It is not a simple "Do it and forget it" procedure. It has a profound and lasting effect on who we are and what we think of ourselves. For many women it has a disastrous impact on every aspect of their physical, emotional, and spiritual lives. At the very least, instead of blindly defending abortion as a good thing, we need to admit that the experience of abortion is a tragedy for everyone involved.

In short, we will never heal the division which abortion is causing in our churches by ignoring it. On the other hand, unless it is addressed in just the right way, it is guaranteed to increase resentments, arouse passions, and ultimately push people away from your community.

This booklet, then, is not about confrontation. Instead, it is about addressing the abortion issue in a *healing* and *reconciling* way. We must become diligent in tearing down the walls which make those who have had abortions feel excluded from full participation in our religious communities. We want them to hear a welcoming message of understanding and forgiveness, not the driving-away message of judgment and condemnation.

DEFUSING TENSIONS

Is it possible to speak about abortion in a way which does not antagonize members of your church? Yes.

Is it possible to preach hope and healing after abortion without risk of encouraging it, or angering pro-lifers? Of course it is.

Is it possible to lead a congregation to greater compassion for *both* the women who have had abortions *and* the unborn children who die from abortion? Absolutely.

Drawing on 14 years of experience in working with women and men who have had abortions, and extensive experience in speaking to mixed crowds of pro-life and pro-choice supporters, I want to share with you what I have learned about opening hearts and defusing the emotional anger surrounding the abortion issue. It is possible to do all of the above, and more. And it's really not that hard to do.

All it takes is an understanding of what drives women to choose abortion and what they experience afterward. By being "inside" their minds, you can speak to what they already know and have experienced. You can show that you understand them, and through this rapport give them the confidence they need to become fully reconciled with themselves, their community, and God.

At the same time, by sharing this understanding with your congregation, you will help the whole community to better understand: (1) the immense pressures women face when they choose abortion; (2) the self-doubt, fears and guilt they face after abortion; and (3) their desire to be understood and forgiven. This understanding will create a more healing environment—and a less judgmental one.

OUR LONG-RANGE GOAL

Our goal is simple. We want to create a society which is more conducive to post-abortion healing. We want to make our society both more pro-life and more pro-woman. And the place to begin this revolution is within the church. Who better than our pastors can, and should, promote healing and reconciliation? Who better than our pastors can help people to better understand themselves and others?

Surveys at abortion clinics have shown that 70 percent of women choosing abortion believe abortion is morally wrong. They are choosing *against* their consciences because of some pressure, from others or circumstances, which makes them feel they have no other choice. Because these women have violated their own moral ideals, it is not surprising that the majority of women and men who have chosen abortion feel guilt and regret about their decision.

These same women and men, however, also fear condemnation and judgment. So it is very common for them to live quietly with their pain, trying to hide from the world their "deep, dark secret." Others are constantly on edge, ready to lash out in resentment against all those who "don't understand" what they have been through.

We need to reach out to these people with a message of hope and understanding. They desperately need to be freed from the shame which holds them back from fully participating in the joy of Christ's forgiveness. But they need us to make the first move, and it must be a move which encourages hope without increasing their fears of condemnation.

ADJUSTING THIS MATERIAL TO YOUR PERSPECTIVE

No matter what your views are on abortion, or what your religious tradition, this booklet will be useful to you and we encourage you to adapt it to your needs.

This booklet is prepared from what is clearly a Christian and biblical perspective. But the basic messages of reconciliation, hope, and community support are common to all faiths and can easily be adapted for use in any religious tradition.

This booklet is also prepared from a pro-life perspective; indeed it is a major part of our pro-woman/pro-life initiative. Our ultimate goal is to create a pro-life society where abortion will be unthinkable, yet forgivable. We want our young women and men to know that abortion is a terrible, self-destructive choice. But we also want them to know that those who have had an abortion, for any reason, will always be welcomed back to their religious communities with understanding and compassion. We never want shame to prevent anyone from seeking, finding, and *experiencing* God's forgiveness.

But while our perspective is informed by a strong pro-life view, we believe these materials will be extremely useful even to ministers who have a strong pro-choice perspective and believe that abortion is morally justified in some, if not many, cases.

We ask pro-choice ministers to be aware of the need of many people in their congregations for post-abortion reconciliation. Whether or not you feel their abortions were morally justified, many of them do not—at least not fully. They do not need more nuanced explanations defending their choice; they need the assurance that God is offering them forgiveness. They need the assurance that their community will not reject them. They need the assurance that it is O.K. to cry and grieve for the children who are now lost to them.

In addition, if you are a pro-choice minister and you want to spare women the judgmentalism of some pro-life advocates, you need to educate your congregation about the immense pressures which drive women to have abortions. You need to create the empathy and humility which leads one to say, "There, but for the grace of God, go I." Even from a pro-choice perspective, it is not necessary to convince pro-lifers that abortion is moral. It is sufficient to convince them that women who abort are not evil haters of life. They are fallible human beings just like the rest of us who make difficult, confused, and often regrettable decisions every day of our lives.

In brief, this booklet is intended to help teach a greater understanding of the abortion experience in order to build bridges between those who are pro-life and those who are pro-choice, and especially between those who have had abortions and those who have not. The result, we believe, will be a society which is more forgiving and more committed to preventing the "need" for

abortion through a more active outreach to the men and women
faced with problem pregnancies.

AN OVERVIEW OF OUR APPROACH

The Jericho Plan is a multi-step process which includes the following steps:

1. Increasing the congregation's empathy with and compassion
   for post-aborted women;

2. Reducing the defensiveness of those involved in abortion and
   stimulating their desire to be understood;

3. Educating the congregation about the many symptoms of
   post-abortion trauma, including its destructive effects on the
   lives of women, men, and families;

4. Explaining how and why denial and avoidance behaviors are
   obstacles to healing which prolong psychological and spiritual suffering;

5. Building up confidence in the post-aborted that they will be
   understood, accepted, and supported by their community;

6. Stimulating the desire for emotional and spiritual healing;
   and,

7. Encouraging reconciliation with God through acknowledgment of one's personal responsibility for the abortion(s) and
   inviting participation in post-abortion recovery programs.

It is doubtful that all of these steps can be accomplished in a
single sermon. Indeed, any attempt to do so would probably be
rushing a process that really takes time. We suggest a series of at
least three sermons.

The first sermon would address steps one and two. It would be
directed principally at the congregation in general so that post-
aborted members of the congregation would see that others are
being called upon to understand them.

The second sermon would cover steps three and four, which
present a closer look at the ongoing effects of abortion in the lives
of women, men, and their families. This sermon reinforces empa-

thy with the emotional hardships faced by post-aborted persons while at the same time encouraging post-aborted members of the congregation to begin to recognize some of the ways in which unresolved issues about their abortions continue to weigh upon their lives.

Lastly, the third sermon completes the cycle by calling on the community to create a non-judgmental and healing environment for their post-aborted brothers and sisters, by stimulating the hope for acceptance and full recovery in the hearts of the post-aborted, and by offering continued support through post-abortion recovery programs offered through the church or outside agencies.

In all of these sermons, it should be stressed, we are never seeking to justify abortion. Instead, we are simply trying to promote a greater understanding of why people choose abortion, even when it goes against their conscience, and to show how this experience of sin has ongoing negative effects on their lives.

This booklet contains much more material than you would need for three sermons. It includes a psychological profile of women who have had abortions, and the testimonies of numerous women, including those who felt forced into unwanted abortions, those who did what they thought was right and necessary at the time but have now discovered a need for God's forgiveness, and those who found healing through Christ and through the compassion of their community. It includes facts, research findings, theological analysis, and biblical words of mercy. Drawing on these resources, you will easily be able to develop sermons which reflect your own style and address your particular community's needs.

CHAPTER ONE

FOCUSING ON WOMEN

PRO-LIFERS believe that the rights of the unborn child must prevail over the desires of the woman. In at least a few cases, this adversarial position has resulted in an exaggerated focus exclusively on the unborn child. A few pro-lifers even believe any effort to focus public attention on the physical and emotional consequences of abortion on women undercuts the moral high ground of opposing abortion simply because all human life is sacred.

Unfortunately, there are more than a few anti-abortionists who have very little sympathy for women who suffer post-abortion problems. Some have even expressed their disdain for women injured by abortion with comments such as, "They deserve what they get."

Less punitive pro-lifers are simply idealists. They want to believe that somehow, with just a better education program, or a more articulate argument, we will be able to awaken America to the moral superiority of our position. To advance this moral argument, evidence of fetal development is relevant but scarred uteruses and tear-filled nights are not.

It is my goal in this chapter to show that the pro-woman approach is not only consistent with the pro-life moral imperative, it is in fact a fuller and more complete expression of it.

THE NATURAL ORDER OF THINGS

We begin with a very simple observation. In God's ordering of creation, it is only the mother who can nurture her unborn child. All that the rest of us can do, then, is to nurture the mother. To help a child, we *must* help the child's mother.

There is nothing startling about this observation. Crisis pregnancy centers have known this truth, and have been living it out, for decades. But we must explore this insight more deeply to understand all that it can teach us.

God has created a connection between a mother and her children that is so deeply personal and intimate that the welfare of each is dependent on the other. As every mother knows from personal experience, this interdependence is for both good and ill. When a mother's children are joyful, their joy lifts her heart. When they are troubled by sorrow, their sorrows weigh on her as well. This principle can be summed up in the following truism: *One cannot help a child without helping the mother; one cannot hurt a child without hurting the mother*.

This is why, from a natural law perspective, we can know in advance that abortion is inherently harmful to women. It is simply impossible to rip a child from the womb of a mother without tearing out a part of the woman herself—a part of her heart, a part of her joy, a part of her maternity.

One does not need to be a "biased" pro-life Christian to see this truth. Consider the testimony of Dr. Julius Fogel, a psychiatrist and obstetrician who has been a long-time advocate of abortion and has personally performed over 20,000 abortions. According to Dr. Fogel:

> Every woman—whatever her age, background or sexuality—has a trauma at destroying a pregnancy. A level of humanness is touched. This is a part of her own life. When she destroys a pregnancy, she is destroying herself. There is no way it can be innocuous. One is dealing with the life force. It is totally beside the point whether or not you think a life is there. You cannot deny that something is being created and that this creation is physically happening....
> Often the trauma may sink into the unconscious and never surface in the woman's lifetime. But it is not as harmless and casual an event as many in the pro-abortion crowd insist. A psychological price is paid. It may be alienation; it may be a pushing away from human warmth, perhaps a hardening of the maternal instinct. Something happens on the deeper levels of a woman's consciousness when she destroys a pregnancy. I know that as a psychiatrist.[1]

---

[1] Colman McCarthy, "A Psychological View of Abortion," *St. Paul Sunday Pioneer Press*, March 7, 1971. Dr. Fogel, who did 20,000 abortions over the subsequent decades, reiterated the same view in a second interview with McCarthy in 1989, in which he disagreed with the Koop report. "The Real Anguish of Abortions," *The Washington Post*, Feb. 5, 1989.

If there is a single principle, then, which lies at the heart of the pro-woman/pro-life agenda, it would have to be this: *The best interests of the child and the mother are **always** joined.*

This is true even if the mother does not initially realize it, and even if she needs a tremendous amount of love and help to see it. Thus, the only way that we can help either the mother or her child is to help both. Conversely, if we hurt either, we hurt both.

This is not an optional truth. It reflects God's ordering of creation. This principle is so important that I must repeat it again: *Only the mother can nurture her unborn child. All that the rest of us can do is to nurture and protect the mother.*

Saving the unborn, then, is a natural byproduct of helping women. Conversely, we can never hope to succeed in our efforts to protect the unborn without first and foremost protecting women. Brute-force bans on abortion will not create a pro-life society. But helping mothers through an aggressive defense of women's *legitimate* rights will.

It is in this very same sense that Pope John Paul II has insisted that it is necessary for those who oppose abortion to become "courageously 'pro-woman,'" promoting a choice that is truly in favor of women. It is precisely the woman, in fact, who pays the highest price, not only for her motherhood, but even more for its destruction, for the suppression of the life of the child who has been conceived. The only honest stance ... is that of *radical solidarity with the woman*."[2] [Italics added.]

LEARNING OUR LESSONS, TOO

Many pro-lifers scratch their heads in confusion, wondering, "How can God have allowed this to go on so long?" So many millions have died, and we seem no closer to converting our nation than we were 20 years ago. When will God stop this holocaust?

This is an important question. As Christians, we believe that from every evil happening, God can resurrect something good— at the very least, repentance and a change of spirit, and often much more. And because the onslaught of abortion is so terrible,

[2] John Paul II, *Crossing the Threshold of Hope* (New York: Alfred A. Knopf, 1994), 207.

we must pray with hope that there is an awful lot of good which God intends to resurrect from this great evil. Greater respect for the unborn and for the sanctity of life is one lesson which our society is certainly intended to learn, but it is by no means the only lesson we are meant to learn.

I believe that at least some of us are so focused on what others need to learn that we are neglecting to see what God may be asking *us* to learn. In short, before we can help others to see, we may still need to extract a plank or two from our own eyes. I honestly believe that, short of Christ's return, God will not bring an end to the abortion holocaust until we Christians learn all that we are meant to learn, namely: greater compassion for sinners.

Compassion for the Pregnant Woman

Pro-lifers have clearly done a tremendous job in the last two decades promoting a more charitable understanding of women who are pregnant out of wedlock. But there is clearly much more that must be done. Churches, families, friends, and employers must make even greater efforts to be supportive of every pregnant woman or single parent, no matter how the child was conceived.

There is no denying the fact that, in previous decades, righteous and judgmental Christians discriminated against and shamed women who were pregnant out-of-wedlock. And it is equally true that this condemning attitude shamed, and continues to shame, many women into seeking abortions. For this, we too share in the guilt of abortion.

If we are to be truly Christian, we must strive to live by and promote the principle that every pregnancy, every birth, is a gift from God. No matter how the pregnancy occurred, no matter what the physical gifts or handicaps of the child, *every child* is a blessing from God, an opportunity and challenge to follow Him in the way of love. When this gift is received by an unmarried couple, it is accompanied by the message that now is the time to become mature and responsible adults. The gift of their child is an opportunity to reform their lives, an opportunity which is built on the demand that they make a commitment to love and serve someone other than themselves: their child. Such couples, then, are given children not as a punishment for fornication, but as a cure for fornication.

As a Christian community, we must cherish life and charitably invite others to seek God's will in their lives. To do this, we must believe that every child is a gift from God and emphatically spread this message. Therefore, the birth of every child should be an *occasion of joy*, not of shame.

Similarly, without ever granting approval to fornication (which causes its own long list of social injuries), we must remind our flock that pre-marital intercourse is not the greatest of sins, much less an unforgivable one. Embarrassed young girls announcing a pregnancy to their parents do not need to be reminded of their mistakes—of which they are already too pointedly aware—so much as reminded that God is now calling upon them to grow up. They need to know that we, their families, their church, and their society, want to continue to help them along that path, over which we too must struggle.

During the last 20 years, Christians have truly come a long way in learning this first lesson. But it is doubtful that we would have learned it if we had not been shocked into greater compassion for young pregnant women out of our concern for their unborn children, who are threatened by abortion. Nonetheless, the witnessing work of our many crisis pregnancy centers and the compassion of so many parents toward their single mother/daughters are evidence that this lesson is being learned.

Let us pray that it is never forgotten.

Compassion for the Post-Aborted

As a Christian community, however, we are not as far along in learning the lesson of compassion toward those who have actually been involved in abortion. Many good-hearted people continue to recoil in horror at anyone who could "kill her baby." They wonder, what kind of monster could do such a thing? For many, judgmentalism comes much easier than compassion because they lack insight into the tremendous pressures and feelings of despair which lead to abortion.

This is the second lesson which we must learn from the abortion holocaust *before* we can expect to conquer it. We must learn that abortion is an act of despair. It is not something women do with vindictive hearts. It is something they do when they feel trapped and helpless. Over *70 percent* of women undergoing abortion

believe it is morally wrong. They are acting *against* their consciences because they feel they have no other choice.

This is one way in which books like *Aborted Women, Silent No
More* have helped to increase the understanding of pro-lifers. By
reading the stories of women who have had abortions and by seeing what drives them to choose abortion, pro-lifers are learning
more and more that "there, but for the grace of God, go I." This
understanding is the basis for acceptance and compassion.
During the last 12 years, this understanding has finally estab-
lished a firm foothold within the pro-life movement, but it is still
far from being universal among Christians in general.

This issue, too, will be discussed at length in the following
chapters. Let it suffice for now to say that Christians must refrain
from condemning and judging the women and men who have
been involved in abortions. Judging them will not free them from
the shame and guilt they already feel. Instead, we must concentrate on sharing with them the hope of God's great mercy. To do
this effectively, we must give them more than our words; we
must give them our hearts.

WHO CAN BEST SPEAK FOR THE UNBORN?

The middle majority of Americans believe that abortion is
wrong, but they also believe that it should be legal, at least in
some cases. There are many things that can be said about this
mindset,[3] but for now it is enough to say that they are uneasy
pragmatists. While they firmly believe that abortion is the killing
of a human being, they also believe it is sometimes necessary and
almost always beneficial to the woman.

Because the middle majority are uncomfortable with the truth
about abortion, they have a psychological need to push out of
their minds any arguments or evidence on behalf of the unborn.

When presented with evidence, such as pictures of the unborn,
whether charmingly angelic or horridly dismembered, they are
likely to resent pro-lifers for rubbing their noses into a truth
which they already know but have deliberately chosen to ignore.

---

[3] See Reardon, *Making Abortion Rare* (Springfield, IL: Acorn Books, 1996),
Chapter Two.

For such people, exposure to pictures of the unborn may serve to solidify their calloused attitudes because it forces them to repeatedly exercise their pattern of denial. This may be why the millions of dollars spent on showing pictures of the unborn to the public have not brought about the mass conversion of hearts for which pro-lifers have frequently, and naively, hoped.

In other words, when hearts are closed, pounding heads with proofs of the unborn child's humanity is ineffective. The truth must enter in a roundabout way, through the testimony of women who grieve over their lost children. Since the middle majority are open to the concerns of women, they will empathize with the grief of post-aborted women, and, in so doing, they will be drawn into implicitly acknowledging the unborn for whom the tears are wept.

Clearly, the most powerful witnesses for the humanity of the unborn are not scientists, but mothers who mourn. All can see that these mothers weep not over the destruction of "products of conception" but over the deaths of their children. While pictures of aborted babies may increase the resentment of the middle majority, the tearful stories of women who have paid the terrible price of abortion open eyes and hearts. Wherever facts of fetal biology will not change hearts, facts of familial relationship will: "It was my innocent little daughter who died that day!"

In this very real way, the issue of the unborn child's human rights is not replaced by a focus on post-abortion issues; it is subsumed into it. In the final analysis, the humanity of the unborn child is revealed to be the only explanation for why abortion causes women so much grief and suffering.

Thus, for those of us who have not had an abortion, the best way that we can draw attention to the humanity of the unborn is by drawing attention to the testimony of those who can speak of this loss from personal experience. By our advocacy for women's rights, we draw attention to wounded mothers. By hushing the din of our own cries, we are allowing the grief-filled voices of the unborn babies' mothers and fathers to be heard by all. We are not leaving the unborn voiceless; we are offering their parents the chance to be heard. Indeed, we must demand that they be heard. After all, who is more entitled to speak for their children than they?

Looking at this same issue from another perspective, we must remember that the interests of a mother and her child are permanently intertwined. This means that the morality of abortion is built right into the psychological effects of abortion. Everyone knows that there is no psychological trauma associated with the discarding of menses. But the discarding of an unborn child's life? *That*, as Dr. Fogel reminds us, is inherently traumatic.

Therefore, when we are talking about the psychological complications of abortion, we are implicitly talking about the physical and behavioral symptoms of a moral problem. By focusing public attention on the symptoms of post-abortion trauma, we will inevitably draw the middle majority back to an understanding of the causes of the problem: the injustice of killing unborn children and the guilt of weakness and betrayal which haunts the hearts of post-aborted mothers and fathers.

With much less ferocity, this same guilt is gnawing at the hearts of the middle majority of Americans, who know the truth but have chosen to ignore it. In helping them to recognize the psychological suffering abortion causes women, we will lead them to rediscover the horror of abortion for themselves.

A Pro-Life Lesson Plan

The discussion above is not meant to imply that appeals on behalf of the unborn are never effective. The fact that the middle majority are uneasy with abortion can be used to our advantage. My point, however, is that we are misusing our resources when we press this advantage first. Our first order of business must be to shake their belief that abortion helps women.

The importance of maintaining this sequence cannot be overstated. It is only *after* the dangers of abortion for women are fully understood by the middle majority, not to mention pro-abortion activists, that we can even begin to open their minds and hearts to the unborn child. If women are not being helped, they will ask themselves, then why are we killing their babies?

In a very real sense, this pro-woman/pro-life agenda is nothing more than a "lesson plan" for leading our nation to an understanding of this reality. It is a process which follows the reverse path of the pro-abortion movement.

The pro-abortion movement was born from a social vision which separated the mother's interests from her unborn baby's. If their interests are separate, then there is a potential conflict between the woman's rights and her unborn child's rights, and only one of them can prevail.

We cannot accept any part of this reasoning. We must reject every ideology which frames the abortion issue in terms of a mother versus her child. We are both pro-woman and pro-child.

We believe that we can and should help both the mother and her child. We believe that the legalization of abortion was not an advance for women's rights, but an advance for social engineers and others who are exploiting women in times of personal crisis.

TEACHING MORALITY BY TEACHING SCIENCE

Believers know that God's moral law is not given to us to enslave us, or even to take the fun out of life. It is given to us as a path toward true happiness. Christians rightly anticipate, then, that any advantage gained through violation of the moral law is always temporary; it will invariably be supplanted by alienation and suffering.

This insight gives us an alternative way of evangelizing. Whenever we cannot convince others to acknowledge a moral truth for the love of God, our second-best option is to appeal to their self-interest. If an act is indeed against God's moral law, it will be found to be injurious to our happiness. Thus, if our faith is true, we would expect to find compelling evidence which demonstrates that such acts as abortion, fornication, and pornography lead, in the end, not to happiness and freedom, but to sorrow and enslavement. By finding this evidence and sharing it with others, we bear witness to the protective good of God's law in a way which even unbelievers must respect.

Research and education about the dangers of abortion, then, are not just grist for political reform. They are also leaven for spiritual reform. As people become more aware of all the hardships abortion causes to women, men, siblings, and society, they will begin to respect the wisdom of God's law. They will begin to think, "Maybe all these religious folk weren't so crazy after all. If they were right about this, when every other power in society said they were wrong, maybe they're right about other things, too."

This approach also recognizes another fundamental aspect of human nature: where there is no love of God, there is an exaggerated love of self. As a corollary to this truth, we should also recognize that wherever there is only self-love, appeals to self-sacrifice will fail, and only appeals to self-preservation can possibly succeed. Often, our warnings will be rejected. But even in these cases, by giving people the warning, we are planting the seeds for repentance and belief when they inevitably hit bottom. This is another reason why we should never be focused on condemning those who are considering or have had abortions. Instead, we should be focused on warning them and offering them mercy.

SUMMARY

The pro-woman/pro-life strategy, which places defense of women's rights at the center of our national debate, is justified by the fact that in God's ordering of creation, only an unborn child's mother can nurture her child; all that we can do is to nurture and protect the mother. Focusing on women's rights is also necessary if we, who want to live as Christians, are to better learn the ways of mercy and compassion.

In focusing attention on post-aborted women, we are actually allowing their voices to be better heard. It is *their* witness on behalf of their unborn, not ours, which will soften hearts and open eyes. In this sense, by focusing on women's rights, we are not ignoring the unborn but, instead, are preparing the stage for the most compelling advocates of all for the unborn—their mothers and fathers.

Our pro-woman/pro-life strategy is actually a lesson plan for educating our nation about how the interests of a mother and her child are inextricably intertwined. One cannot hurt a child without hurting the child's mother, and this is especially true in the case of abortion. As people learn this, they will not only reopen their hearts to the unborn, they will reopen their hearts to the beauty of God's moral law.

None of what I have presented in this chapter is novel, as is demonstrated by a letter which Dr. O. E. Worcester wrote to the

Journal of the American Medical Association over 100 years ago. Dr. Worcester wrote to complain against her male colleagues who treated women who were pregnant out-of-wedlock with great disrespect. Worst of all, she insisted, these same physicians willingly added to the guilt of these used and abandoned women by giving them abortions rather than true compassionate aid. When a colleague asked her to help perform abortions, she refused, saying, "I loved woman too well to help her add murder to her other sin. If mother love and the touch of baby fingers did not save her to God and womanhood, nothing could. That it could, I had proof in many cases where forsaken mothers had, in spite of all, carved for themselves and their fatherless children an honorable place in the world."

Dr. Worcester concluded her reprimand of her colleagues with a pointed condemnation of misogynist abortionists, an appeal to the inseparability of woman and child, and a plea for true compassion:

I have never seen cause to hold the male element less responsible for the slaughter of the innocents than in the days of Herod. Then, as now, men seem to fear the coming of Christ born of woman....

This is my plea: "What God hath joined together, let not man put asunder," in the medical profession or elsewhere.

Let men and women join forces under the banner of Him who said: "He that is without sin among you, let him first cast a stone at her," and also: "Neither do I condemn thee; go and sin no more."

Let us join forces all along the line, and fight this hydraheaded monster to the death and save our nation.[4]

To this plea I can add only one word: Amen.

[4] O.E. Worcester, M.D., "From A Woman Physician: An Open Letter to Dr. W.W. Parker," *JAMA* 22:599, 1894, reprinted in "JAMA 100 Years Ago," *JAMA* 271(15), April 20, 1994.

CHAPTER TWO

AN OVERVIEW OF OUR HEALING STRATEGY

No one is proud of having had an abortion. We can be proud, or at least unashamed, of our right to speak freely in public, of our right to vote, of our right to sit at the front or back of the bus, or of any other authentic right. But no one is proud of having an abortion. For everyone involved, the experience of abortion is associated with shame. Even for those who are convinced that it was the morally right thing to do, it is touched at least by the embarrassment that they made the unenlightened "mistake" of becoming pregnant.

For the women and men who have had abortions, their first impulse is to bury their doubts and pain, to pack them away in a box marked "The Past—Do Not Open." They are determined to focus on the future. If they do not succeed at this, and the physical, psychological, or spiritual effects of abortion become so severe that they can no longer be denied or ignored, their second impulse is to believe that they deserve to suffer for what they have done.

This is one of the ways in which abortion is like rape. Both rapists and abortionists injure women in a way which creates so much shame that their victims actually help to conceal the crime. Furthermore, the victims of rape and abortion are both inclined to blame themselves for the "stupidity" of having put themselves into the hands of the one who injured them.

REMOVING THE PLANK FROM OUR OWN EYE

Before we can develop a healing environment for others, it is essential that we first heal ourselves. We, the pro-life movement and the Church, must learn to replace any traces of judgmental-

13

ism with compassion, prejudice with understanding. We must learn to see those who have undergone abortions not as different from ourselves, but as identical to ourselves. We must find the humility to see that without the overflowing grace of God, under the right conditions and the right pressures, we too would be capable of abortion, if not worse.

We also need to remember that our concern for unborn children should always be one with our concern for the unborn child's mother. As previously discussed, this is necessary because by God's natural ordering of things, an unborn child can only be nurtured and protected by the mother. All that we can do is to nurture and protect the mother. To make this point in another way, the best way we can live out our concern for the unborn child is through actions taken on behalf of the unborn's mother. It is only in serving her needs that we can serve her child.

From another perspective, while we can and should mourn the deaths of the children killed by abortion, we should really be more concerned about the ravages of abortion on the souls of the women and men who have been touched by this sin. This argument will be elaborated upon further in the next two chapters. For now it is enough to share the insight of a crisis pregnancy counselor who once told me, "When I began this work, I was mostly concerned about the unborn. But after working with so many young girls who have had abortions, what saddens me most is how abortion destroys the joy of their youth, and strips away every last shred of their innocence. Nothing can make a young girl feel more worthless and despicable than having killed her own child."

I sincerely believe that this attitude is the only one which has any hope of creating a pro-life society. By applying generous doses of sympathy, understanding, and charity toward those who have been involved in abortion, we will create a ripple effect which will truly transform the world.

REDUCING JUDGMENTALISM

Women who have had abortions are either filled with humility or shame. The forgiven feel humility; the unforgiven feel shame. The former have found humility in a repentance which requires the acknowledgment of one's guilt, one's weakness, one's flaws. But for many, shame is a manifestation of denial. To protect their denial, many become resentful, defiant, and even hateful of everyone who aggravates the feelings of guilt which they are trying to deny. They feel that no one can understand them, and they fear that everyone is prepared to condemn them.

This is our task then: to reduce feelings of shame by increasing our own level of understanding and compassion. Through compassion, we seek to eliminate the hurdles women and men face along the way to repentance. This is the path they must travel in the search for post-abortion healing. It is therefore extremely important for the pro-woman/pro-life movement to concentrate its public relations efforts on counteracting the image that pro-lifers are judgmental and replace it with a message of understanding and compassion. This message must be prominent in all of our campaigns, but it must especially be proclaimed in our churches.

We are calling upon you, our clergy, to give entire sermons on the need for understanding and compassion for those who have had abortions. This can be done without in any way condoning abortion. Using as examples the testimonies of women who have chosen abortion, congregations can be reminded of how, in times of great stress, people do even those things which they most abhor. With examples of women who have been literally dragged to unwanted abortions, and those who simply gave in under the weight of many pressures, people should be helped to see that women are not always fully culpable. This does not lessen the seriousness of abortion, but it does lessen our tendency to judge and blame.

Church communities need to be reminded that we need not judge why people have had abortions—they will do that for themselves, perhaps more harshly than we would. Nor do we need to dwell on the humanity of the child or the sinfulness of abortion, because these truths are implicitly known by all who have been involved in abortion. Whether they acknowledge their sinfulness or defend their abortions as "necessary," everyone, on some level, knows the truth of what happened. A life was destroyed.

The knowledge that the human fetus, the human embryo, or even the human zygote, is in fact a *human being* is as undeniable as the answer to the child's question: "Where do babies come from?" While a child might be temporarily diverted from the answer to this question, no child's curiosity is completely satisfied until the full truth is revealed. Life begins at conception. Babies are created by the uniting (hopefully in an act of love) of a man and woman, the sharing of the substance of two selves becoming one in the flesh—both symbolically, in the sexual act, and most truly, in the conception of a new life. Every adult remembers when they learned this amazing truth as a child. Everyone's biology bears constant witness to it. And it is this truth, no matter how much one tries to ignore it, forget it, or bury it beneath slogans or philosophical quibbles—it is this truth, that makes *everyone* uneasy with abortion.

For many, this is a truth which they dare not look upon. Attempts to force them to confront it only aggravate anxiety, fear, resentment, and anger. In short, walls go up. On the other hand, showing that we have learned what abortion does to women, and men, makes walls come down because *this* is what they know, *this* is what they feel and have experienced. The knowledge that one's church community understands what one has experienced is itself healing.

BUILDING BRIDGES WITH EMPATHY

Through this approach of taking down walls of defensiveness, post-aborted women and men can be led to the truth they most desperately need, the truth about forgiveness. They need to hear that in repentance and reform, there is freedom and new life, even after suffering the greatest of shames. They need to discover hope in the message of our non-condemning acceptance of them as our brothers and sisters. After all, since Christ Himself is offering them forgiveness, who are we to cast the first stone? In short, the message of forgiveness must always precede the message of life's sanctity, for it is only after they feel forgiveness, or at least taste its hope, that post-aborted women and men can bear to look directly at the truth about their unborn children.

To succeed in creating a healing environment, we must begin by teaching others how to understand their pangs of doubt, their ambivalence, their grief. In the process, we will also be helping the post-aborted members of our churches to understand their own confused and buried feelings. Even if some post-aborted members cannot admit having had these feelings themselves, they will immediately recognize that what we are saying must be true at least for "others." This is very important, for by even this small step of admitting that the pain of "others" is real, they are opening a door through which they may eventually recognize their own need to heal buried feelings of remorse.

Most of all, we, their church community, must be ready to cry with those who are aware of their loss. We must graciously acknowledge their need and desire for healing and share with them the certainty of God's freely offered forgiveness. We must assure them that our faith does not condemn any of us to a life of shame. All of us are sinners, but through God's mercy, all of us can find peace again.

A HEALING ENVIRONMENT BUILDS STRENGTH

By our promise of compassion we break the bonds of shame which are an obstacle to repentance. In this way, by creating a more healing environment, we will be encouraging more people to seek post-abortion healing. In helping post-aborted women and men to move beyond denial, resentment, and shame, we will also be helping them to become active witnesses for the sanctity of life. This is a good end in and of itself. But it is also good for the Church and the pro-life movement.

The psychological and spiritual healing which can follow an abortion is never automatic. As with all healings of the spirit, it is always the result of the Lord's initiative and the sinner's response in faith, including sincere regret, a change of heart, and acceptance of God's forgiveness.

Those who experience post-abortion healing strengthen the Church. In finding forgiveness, they find humility and a restoration of their faith. Many become deeply spiritual. Having experienced the depths of despair, they become marvelous witnesses to hope.

They also strengthen the pro-life cause. They are the voice of experience, the unimpeachable witnesses of abortion's dangers. As readers of their stories know, there is no more powerful testimony on behalf of the unborn, in condemnation of abortion's exploitation of women, and in the appeal for social and political reform than the testimony of post-aborted women.[1]

TOWARD CRITICAL MASS

In physics, critical mass is the point at which a fusion reaction takes place and becomes self-perpetuating. I pray for the day when the post-abortion healing movement will reach "critical mass." At that point, there will be an explosion of interest in, and demand for, post-abortion healing services. On that day, public empathy for post-aborted women and men will have overcome the pro-abortion bias against "traitors" who speak out against abortion. On that day, movie stars, athletes, politicians, and other public figures will be able to publicly confess their guilt over past abortions and proclaim their healing to others without fear of destroying their careers. Everywhere, the witness of post-aborted men and women will be leading others to seek and accept post-abortion healing.

Still another aspect of post-abortion healing which should not be missed is its impact on family members. Many people remain silent about abortion in general because they do not want to hurt loved ones who they know have had abortions. But when these loved ones begin to witness to the grief abortion has caused in their lives, this same loyalty among family members which previously fostered silence will now encourage them to speak up and support reform. This effect should not be underestimated. For every woman who has had an abortion, there are numerous people who remain neutral on abortion, or hide their pro-life sympathies, out of deference to her feelings. Every post-aborted woman who is healed brings with her new allies in our battle. This is our key to a broad segment of the middle majority who are presently avoiding involvement in the abortion debate.

SUMMARY

Millions of men and women silently carry the grief of a secret abortion in their hearts. They are silenced by shame. They are

---

[1] For examples of their testimonies, see *The Post-Abortion Review*, *Aborted Women, Silent No More*, and *Real Choices*.

silenced by the belief that they are alone and no one can understand their pain. Indeed, they fear that "it's just something wrong with me. No one else feels this way after an abortion."

These walking wounded need to learn that we do understand. They need to know that it is normal and necessary not only to grieve after an abortion, but also to seek emotional and spiritual healing. It is our obligation, as Christians, to help them escape their feelings of shame and to find peace in God's forgiveness. Most of all, we must help them to forgive themselves.

It is critical, therefore, that the pro-life movement and the Church break through the media-imposed image that we are judgmental and condemning of those who have had abortions. Our rhetoric must hold fast to the defense of the twin truths of the sacredness of human life and God's love for all sinners, among whom we number ourselves. Perhaps we should invest in bumper stickers which read, "Abortion always Kills. God will always Forgive."

We need to overcome the fear of some pro-lifers that, if we stress God's forgiveness, we will be encouraging women to abort now and seek forgiveness later. I believe this is an unwarranted fear which stifles the display of understanding and compassion which is truly needed to create an environment conducive to post-abortion healing. It is only through such a healing environment that we will finally build a pro-life society. Only then, when the grief and suffering abortion causes to women, men, families, and society are known by all, will abortion be not only illegal, but unthinkable.

CHAPTER THREE

CONQUERING DESPAIR

ABORTION is an act of despair. *Despair is not only the driving force behind most abortion choices, it is also the greatest obstacle to post-abortion recovery.* Until pro-lifers understand this, they will never be effective at helping women who are faced with the abortion choice—or are trying to recover from the abortion choice.

In describing the despair which leads women to abort, Frederica Mathewes-Green of Feminists for Life of America gives us this compelling word-picture: "No woman wants an abortion as she wants an ice cream cone or a Porsche. She wants an abortion as an animal caught in a trap wants to gnaw off its own leg."[1]

This quote is so powerfully accurate that it has even been reprinted by Planned Parenthood. Why? Because pro-abortionists have long wanted to diffuse the notion that women abort for selfish or casual reasons. They want the public to sympathize with the desperation of women seeking abortions because they want to convert sympathy for women into support for abortion.

Actually, the fact that most women agonize over the decision to abort is one of the few areas for finding "common ground" in the abortion debate. Most, if not all, counselors and researchers, on both sides of the political issue, would agree that most abortion decisions involve elements of fear and despair.

But simply because a woman agonizes over an abortion decision does not make the decision morally acceptable, not even to the women themselves. In fact, post-abortion research suggests that the more a woman agonizes over making an abortion decision, the more she is likely to agonize over the abortion afterwards. Maternal desires, moral doubts, and feelings of being exploited do not disappear after an abortion. They continue. They grow.

---

[1] Frederica Mathewes-Green, *Real Choices* (Sisters, OR: Multnomah Books, 1994), 19. *Real Choices* is another excellent book examining the pressures which push women into unwanted abortions.

They become sources of constant reflection or stifling avoidance. They can even become the source of a crippling self-condemnation.

ESCAPE THROUGH SELF-DESTRUCTION

Returning to Mathewes-Green's analogy of an animal gnawing its leg off to escape a trap, we see that abortion is actually an act of self-destruction. Remember how Dr. Julius Fogel, a psychiatrist and obstetrician who has personally performed over 20,000 abortions also described it this way: "Every woman...has a trauma at destroying a pregnancy....This is a part of her own life. When she destroys a pregnancy, she is destroying herself."

When pro-abortionists view a woman in this desperate situation, their solution is to offer the woman a clean, legal way of "cutting off the offending leg." But what abortion counselors fail to tell women who are choosing abortion is that the loss of their "leg" will leave them crippled. Like many amputees, they will experience the feeling of a "phantom leg." This missing part will leave them less whole and less capable. And at times this missing piece will cause an indescribable ache and a flood of uncontrollable tears. In escaping the trap, they will have lost a part of themselves.

Contrast this approach to that of crisis pregnancy centers where pro-lifers are committed to finding a way to open the jaws of the trap to save both the woman and her "leg." Pro-lifers insist that there is always room for hope. There is always a way to avoid a destructive amputation—a way which, in the long run, will be appreciated by both her and her "leg."

What we see in these two perspectives is the difference between despair and hope. Despair inevitably leads us to accept abortion. Hope always leads us to embrace life.

Hope is a virtue. It is centered on God, the source of all hope. Despair is a sin against hope. It is one of Satan's greatest weapons.

THE WEAPON OF DESPAIR

Despair involves a loss of faith and trust in God. In the case of abortion, the desperate woman has lost faith in the promise that God has a plan for her life and a plan for her child's life.

Desperate people try to take control. They try to save whatever they can by doing whatever needs to be done—which may include betraying their own values. For example, when the Nazis undertook the extermination of millions of Jews, the sheer magnitude of their task required them to develop ways of soliciting the cooperation of the victims. There were too few soldiers to contain millions of rebellious Jews. So it was necessary to manipulate their victims so that they would choose to cooperate for at least one day at a time. The Nazis did this by exposing the Jews to *limited* threats; the victims were always left with the bit of hope that by submitting to the present indignity, there was something else which could be saved. According to sociologist Zygmunt Bauman:

> At all stages of the Holocaust, the victims were *confronted with a choice* (as least subjectively—even when objectively the choice did not exist any more, having been pre-empted by the secret decision of physical destruction). They could not choose between good and bad situations, but they could at least choose between greater and lesser evil....In other words, they *had something to save*. To make their victims' behavior predictable and hence manipulable and controllable, the Nazis had to induce them to act in the "rational mode." To achieve that effect, they had to make the victims believe that there was indeed something to save, and that there were clear rules as to how one should go about saving it.[2]

These choices were presented in a way that discouraged reflecting on the decisions from a moral perspective. Instead, the victims were pressured to make *rational* decisions based on the rational need to "save whatever we can."

Using this demonic strategy, the Nazis encouraged the empowerment of Jewish ghetto leaders who would see to the needs of the people, coordinate distribution of medicine and materials, maintain morale, etc. These same leaders were then manipulated into cooperating with the Nazi extermination program. They were confronted with the agonizing choice of cooperating with the Nazis or witnessing the slaughter of their people. At first, the cooperation was in "small" things, maintaining a ghetto police force, providing lists of names, selection of ghetto residents to be sent to "resettlement" projects, providing transportation to pick-up

---

[2] Zygmunt Bauman, *Modernity and the Holocaust* (Ithaca, NY: Cornell University Press, 1989), 130.

points, and the like. In some cases, when the Nazis wanted to
punish the entire community for some infraction, Jewish leaders
were even forced to select and arrest the desired number of victims
who were to be publicly executed by the Nazis. And always, no
matter what the request, the leaders were told that by cooperating
they were saving the lives of the majority who remained. Leaders
who didn't cooperate were eliminated. Leaders who did cooperate
saved their own lives and those of their families, at least for a time,
and were left to agonize over their complicity.

The similarity between Nazi manipulations of the Jews and the
abortionists' manipulation of women faced with crisis pregnancies
is striking. Just as the Jews were forced to choose between losing
everything or "just a little," so abortion counselors encourage the
victim-woman to view "this pregnancy" as a threat to everything
she has—her relationships, her family, her career, her entire future.
She is assured that by sacrificing this one thing (a tiny unborn
child), she can save the rest. During this process, the victim-
woman is urged to view the abortion decision not as a moral
choice, but as a rational choice of "saving what you can."

But in fact, just as those who reluctantly cooperated with the
Nazis discovered, the bargain is a false one. The demands on
ghetto leaders to sacrifice more and more victims never stopped.
And so it is with the post-aborted woman. After her child is
destroyed, she faces self-condemnation, lower self-esteem, difficulty with relationships, substance abuse, career problems, a cycle
of repeat abortions, and more. Often she experiences an intense
desire for replacement pregnancies to atone for her lost child, and
she becomes a single parent—the very problem she sought to
avoid in the first place—but now she also has to deal with the
emotional scars of an abortion.

THE DEVIL VERSUS CHRIST

It is significant how differently Christ and the devil appear
before and after any sin, in this case, abortion. Before the abortion,
Christ stands, with his arms outstretched to block the way, saying,
"Do not do this thing. The sacrifices you must make now will be
rewarded a hundred fold. I offer you life, so that you may live life

abundantly. Place your hope in Me and I will not abandon you."

The devil, on the other hand, insists, "You must get rid of it. Look at all you will lose....You have no choice. You have already gotten yourself into this problem. Now you must get yourself out. Do this one thing and then you will be back in the driver's seat of life. Things will be the way they used to be."

Christ asks us to trust in a plan for our future which we do not yet fully understand; Satan urges us to act *now*, to take control, to save what we already have. Christ asks us to make a moral decision rooted in hope; Satan asks us to make a "rational" decision based on present needs, desires, and fears.

But after the abortion, how do they appear? Afterwards, Christ continues to offer hope: "Come to me. I want to share your tears. I want to comfort you. Know that all is forgiven. See, your child is in My arms waiting for you to join us when your day is completed."

Satan, on the other hand, continues to fan the flames of despair. He who pretended to be on her side now stands as her fiercest accuser. "Look at what you have done! You have murdered your own child! Can there be anything worse than that? There's no hope for you now. You are nothing. You're beyond redemption! You may as well seek what little comfort you can in the bottom of a booze bottle, in the silence of suicide, or in the embrace of an affair. And if you get pregnant again, you've already had an abortion once, so you might as well do it again—it may even help you to get tougher and more immune to this pain. It makes no difference now. You've proven you can murder. Nothing can be worse. And, oh, how you must hate those people who led you to this. Your boyfriend, your parents, your doctor. There is no one you can trust. There is no one who can love YOU—*a murderer*. You are alone. Your best hope is to bury your past. Hide it from others. Hide it from yourself. But remember it will always be yours alone to bear."

Before the abortion, Christ condemns it and Satan makes excuses for it. After the abortion, Satan is the one condemning it while Christ wants to forgive it.[3]

---

[3] This general description of the stance of Christ and Satan before and after sin is drawn from the audio-tape "The Devil" by Archbishop Fulton Sheen and is applied here specifically to the case of abortion.

This is the devil's bargain. He encourages women to submit to abortion in order to avoid losing what they already have. But once they have chosen it, he tries to keep them trapped in despair so as to strip away everything else. Indeed, Satan pumps as much despair into their lives as he can generate. And not only into their lives, but into the lives of the child's father, and grandparents, and siblings, and everyone else he can touch with the poison of abortion. His purpose is threefold: to generate misery, to encourage more sin, and to create doubt in the unfathomable mercy of God.

DESPAIR AND FORGIVENESS

For many post-aborted women, the forgiveness of God is a precept which they can mouth, but which is difficult for them to digest. How can *they* be forgiven? The horror of their sin is so great. Many know that they must believe in God's forgiveness, and they do so in an act of faith. But how can they *feel* forgiven, when every instinct in their nature says they cannot be forgiven, even *should not* be forgiven?

I certainly do not have a complete answer to this complex question, but I do believe we can offer more than simply the truth that "God can forgive any sin, even abortion." While this is a revealed truth, it is also a conclusion for which we can develop a greater appreciation if we look at some of the reasons behind this truth. As we look, I believe we will discover not only truths which must be shared with post-aborted men and women, but also truths which explain why our focus must be on ministering to them, not accusing them.

Assume that I am on a joy ride, speeding along for thrills. I see a flash of light. A bump. And I know I've killed someone. I run to the victim. He's dead. An innocent man has been killed because of my negligence. My guilt is very real and well deserved. But a moment later my victim jumps to his feet alive and uninjured. Now the guilt is gone! I am spared, not by my virtue, but by *his* immortality.

In just the same way we have all been forgiven of murder. Because of our sins, of whatever type, each of us is guilty of crucifying Christ. Because of our sins, He was killed on the cross. His blood is on our hands. Yet on Easter Sunday, He rose from the dead. He is not dead at all! The guilt has been lifted.

WORDS TO A GRIEVING MOTHER

"But my child did not rise from the dead," a post-aborted woman complains. "She is truly dead, and I am guilty of her death." But to such a woman I would respond that this is another example of her guilt being twisted into despair.

Death is an experience, not a state of being. For "God is not the God of the dead but of the living. All are alive for Him" (Luke 20:38). When your child was killed by abortion, he or she *experienced* death. But your child is not *dead* in the sense of destroyed. Your child, like us all, is immortal. Death cannot keep her down.

C.S. Lewis explains it well when he writes, "There are no ordinary people. You have never talked to a mere mortal. Nations, cultures, arts, civilization—these are mortal, and their life is to ours as the life of a gnat. But it is immortals whom we joke with, work with, marry, snub and exploit—immortal horrors or everlasting splendors." Damned or glorified, all people live on (Matt. 25:46).

Therefore, like Christ, your child lives. Your guilt can be removed precisely because God has already preserved your child from destruction. He lives! She lives! They all live in Him!

Remember, your abortion was a result of your failure to trust God. In giving you that pregnancy, God was giving you the opportunity to love. But you rejected this gift because you did not trust God's plan for you. This lack of trust and obedience is at the root of all sin, yours and mine. So it is only right that the reparation for abortion is found not by clinging to guilt and despair, but by trusting in God's love. You failed once in rejecting His gift of a new life. But now He has a new plan for you, a second gift which He passionately desires for you—the gift of His forgiveness, the rebirth and renewal of your spirit.

To refuse God's mercy is to refuse His love. Don't insult Him by refusing His forgiveness. Accept God's forgiveness, not because you deserve it, but so that God can use you as an instrument for showing the abundant glory of His mercy. Accepting the gift of

God's forgiveness is actually a humble thing to do. It is your first step toward an obedience which is rooted in both faith and hope, and it is your only escape from the tar pit of despair.

THE WORST EVIL

In a sense (and I write this asking the reader's forbearance for my inability to express this more precisely), since immortal persons cannot be destroyed, the greatest tragedy in killing is what this sin does to killers. This does not deny that the killed have been unjustly deprived of life, but we know that God will be merciful toward these innocent victims. We should be more concerned about the eternal fate of killers.

Even Socrates, a pagan philosopher, recognized that, in terms of preserving the nobility of our character, inner virtue, and our very souls, it is better to suffer evil from others than to do evil ourselves. Specifically, Socrates argued that those who do unjust acts are becoming unjust; those who reject their obligations to others are becoming irresponsible.

Because he believed that moral character was more important than physical well-being, Socrates believed that harm which is done to one's body is less important than harm done to one's "inner self" as the result of immoral choices. In the case of abortion, he would argue, the harm done to the mother's soul is a greater moral evil than the physical wrong suffered by the unborn child, who remains innocent.

There is nothing in this argument which is contrary to Christian thought. Indeed, Scripture teaches not only that it is preferable to suffer evil than to commit evil but that those who suffer from wrongdoing can even rejoice in being called upon to share in the suffering of Christ (1 Peter 4:13-16). As we have suggested above, and will discuss further in the next chapter, the unborn child who suffers physical harm from abortion is an immortal being whose innocence will be recognized and rewarded by God. But the spiritual damage done to those who are involved in abortion, directly or indirectly, individually or socially, is immeasurable.

Let us look at the spiritual meaning of abortion from another perspective. We begin by recognizing the Judeo-Christian teaching that children are always a gift from God. Because God is the author of all life, no child is conceived by accident. Each has a part to play in God's design. This providential purpose includes not only the child's destiny, but the destiny of those whom the child's life touches. For parents, the conception of a child may be intended to lead them to greater generosity, responsibility, and understanding of the meaning of unconditional and sacrificial love. (Even in the case of experimentation on *in vitro* human embryos, God allows these human lives to be conceived so that scientists and the eugenicists who fund them can prove their depravity and thereby justify their final judgment.) No life is created without a purpose. It is our role to simply find and cooperate with that purpose.

Thus, whenever we reject the gift of new life, we are rejecting a gift from *God*! Obviously, this is an insult to the Giver. But it is an insult which will be mercifully forgiven. And, as members of the body of Christ, we are called upon to be mirrors of God's mercy and ambassadors of His forgiveness. While we can do nothing for the unborn children in heaven, there is much we can do for those who have been so spiritually wounded by abortion.

In brief, without in any way diminishing the horror of abortion, I am confident that children killed by abortion are in the enviable position of living in the glorious presence of Christ. Furthermore, if the salvation of souls is the greatest of goods, then the damnation of souls is the greatest of evils. Thus, the greatest evil of abortion lies in the spiritual damage it inflicts on the women, men, and families (and politicians) who are ensnared by it. It is these bleeding, bruised, despairing, and even rebellious souls who are most at risk. It is they to whom Christians need to reach out with the good news of forgiveness and hope.

SUMMARY

The greatest tragedy of abortion is that it separates men and women from God. The despair which drives women to abortion is also used to make them doubt God's mercy, which, in turn, leads to an embracing of atheism. For some sinners, the fear of hell makes them hope for a death of annihilation: "When it's over, it's over." For those trapped by despair, this is their only hope, the annihilation of self. This is why so many post-aborted women

directly seek death through suicide. Others court death's sem-
blance in abusive relationships or the mind-deadening effects of
drug or alcohol abuse. Still others just run from life, burying
themselves in everything from pointless work to joyless parties—
anything that distracts them from reflection.

   Abortion is, of course, not the only sin which separates us from
God. But to those who have had one, it almost always creates the
biggest rift. To return across this chasm, they need our help, offered
graciously and abundantly. In giving them hope, we will be giving
them back to God.

CHAPTER FOUR

TRUSTING GOD'S MERCY FOR UNBORN CHILDREN

THERE is still one more hook of despair which Satan can use to deny peace of mind to the mothers and fathers of aborted children. This is the fear that even if God can forgive them, their unborn children will be deprived of heaven because they were denied baptism.

This fear that unbaptized infants will be denied heaven is also used by Satan to build a wall of separation and prejudice between pro-lifers and post-aborted men and women. Not a few Christians have coldly turned their backs on those who have had abortions, believing that they have deprived God of the souls of their unborn children. They may not wish the post-aborted ill, but they cannot bring themselves to offer them comfort, either.

There are two reasons why the issue of the final repose of the unborn is a very important one, not only for those who seek post-abortion healing, but also for the pro-life movement as a whole. First, if we truly believe that the unborn are in heaven, then anger and resentment will be dissipated. Second, concern for the living, those who suffer the guilt of abortion, will not only be easier, it will be more compelling.

THE ISSUE: THE NECESSITY OF BAPTISM

The question of salvation for the unborn arises from an interpretation of Christ's solemn pronouncement to Nicodemus that "no one can enter into God's kingdom without being begotten of water and the Spirit" (John 3:5). The necessity of baptism is further supported by Christ's statement, "The man who believes in it [the good news] and accepts baptism will be saved; the man who refuses to believe will be condemned" (Mark 16:16). Note,

31

however, that condemnation is pronounced for those who *refuse* to believe. Nothing is said regarding those who have not had the opportunity to believe. Indeed, we are also told that no one will be judged guilty simply because of his or her ignorance (John 9:41).

What are we to make of this, then? Baptism by water is clearly the way God has given the Church for bringing new members into His Body. When it can be done, it ought to be done. However, God's mercy is not limited by human failings, nor are His means limited by the physical reality which defines human interaction. Indeed, it is clear in Scripture that God has at least one other way of bringing sanctifying grace to those who have died without having the opportunity to receive baptism by water.

The most obvious example of unbaptized persons who were saved is that of the Old Testament saints, including the patriarchs, the prophets, and untold others. For the sake of these departed, Christ went in death to preach to them "in prison" (1 Peter 3:19) so that they "might live in the spirit in the eyes of God" (1 Peter 4:6). Yet another example is shown in the good thief, who followed Jesus into Paradise (Luke 23:42-44) without the benefit of baptism by water.

In fact, the Church has always recognized that martyrs who die for the faith before they have the opportunity to be baptized are reborn in a baptism by blood rather than water.[1] Baptism by either water or blood has been recognized as having the same efficacy and the same source. This view was defended by the prominent Christian apologist Tertullian around 203 A.D., who wrote:

> We have one and only one Baptism in accord with the Gospel (Eph. 4:4-6).... [But there is] a second font, one with the former [water]: namely, that of blood, of which the Lord says: "I am to be baptized with a baptism" (Luke 12:50, Mark 10:38-39), when He had already been baptized [by water]. For He had come through water and blood, as John wrote (1 John 5:6), so that He might be baptized with water and glorified with blood. He sent out these two Baptisms from the wound in His pierced side (John 19:34), that we might in like manner be called by water and chosen by blood, and so that they who believed in His blood might be washed by the water. If they might be washed in the water, they must necessarily be so by blood. This is the Baptism which replaces that of the foun-

---

[1] Cyprian, *Letters*, 72[73]:22 (A.D. 255).

tain, *when it has not been received*, and restores it when it has been lost.[2] [Italics added.]

Tertullian's argument that baptism by blood can be a substitute for baptism by water is further supported by the fact that Christ offered the sons of Zebedee the baptism of suffering as one with the cup of salvation (Mark 10:38-39). Furthermore, Scripture tells us that before Christ's death, John's baptism by water was only a baptism of repentance (Acts 19:4, Luke 3:3). It was only after Christ's baptism in blood that the baptism of water was raised up to become a baptism with the Holy Spirit (Acts 1:5, John 16:7).

Clearly, then, the understanding that God has a means to save those who through no fault of their own have been denied the opportunity of baptism by water is not novel. Indeed, it is revealed by Scripture. Therefore, if we are to properly interpret Christ's insistence on baptism by water, we must admit that it is a binding command on the living, while recognizing that this precept does not preclude God from offering some other spiritual means of rebirth for those who die without this opportunity.[3]

GOD'S SPECIAL LOVE FOR CHILDREN

We know as part of our revealed faith that God desires the salvation of all (1 Tim. 2:4, Rom. 8:32) and that his mercy endures forever (Psalm 136). Though all are stained by original sin, all whom Christ claims for Himself will live in Him (1 Cor. 15:22-23). That Christ should not claim the unborn as His own is unimaginable, contrary to both reason and revelation. Furthermore, Paul teaches that God's mercy and providence extend even to the unborn, who have done neither good nor evil (Rom. 9:11), and Christ himself repeatedly expressed His special love of infants and children.

> And they brought unto him also infants, that he would touch them: but when his disciples saw it, they rebuked them. But Jesus called

---

[2] Tertullian, *On Baptism*, 15:1; 16:1-2 (A.D. 203).

[3] What this way is has not been fully revealed. On the other hand, since it is a spiritual baptism which is outside the responsibilities of believers on earth, it is not something about which we need to know the details. It is enough for us to know that it is possible. Once this truth is recognized, we can then confidently trust God's mercy and justice.

them, and said, "Suffer the little children to come unto me, and forbid them not: for of such is the kingdom of God" (Luke 18:15-16).

See how Jesus describes heaven; it is filled with infants such as these! And are not His words a warning against those who would forbid these children entry into His heavenly kingdom? And look at yet another occasion:

[The disciples asked Jesus:] "Who is of greatest importance in the kingdom of God?" He called a little child over and stood him in their midst and said: "I assure you, unless you change and become like little children, you will not enter the kingdom of God....See that you never despise one of these little ones. I assure you, their angels in heaven constantly behold my heavenly Father's face.... Just so, it is no part of your heavenly Father's plan that a single one of these little ones shall ever come to grief" (Matt. 18:1-2, 10, 14).

Other renderings of this last line are that none of these little ones should ever "perish" or be "lost." These passages suggest a promise of universal salvation for the innocents, for (1) they are numbered among those of greatest importance in God's kingdom, (2) their angels pray for them before the Father, and (3) the Father wills that none of them should be lost. Notice also that the small child standing before Christ was unbaptized.

Reason, too, demands our acknowledgment of God's saving grace for the unborn. Christ's love is so great, He died to bring salvation to sinners who deserve nothing (Romans 5:6-9). Yet, if He would save sinners like us, would He not do at least as much, if not more, for the unborn who have not sinned?[4] Of course He would. Those who doubt it must defend the absurd notion that God's judgments are less merciful than human judgments.

THEORIES OF SALVATION

While the method of salvation for the unborn is not revealed, there are some theories which are useful to consider, remembering always that they are only theories. Some Christian theologians

---

[4]This type of *a fortiori* argument, "If Y is true, then how much more likely that Z is true," was frequently used for teaching and theological deduction by Jesus and Paul. See Matt. 7:11, 10:25, 12:12, Luke 11:13, 12:24, 28, Romans 11:12, 24, 1 Cor. 6:3, Heb. 9:14.

speculate that at the moment of death, God enlightens the minds of the "incompetent" so that they can freely choose for or against Him. This possibility would be analogous to the free choice for or against God which the angels made at the time of their creation.

Others believe that children who die without formal baptism, or other incompetents who are incapable of understanding or freely choosing baptism, acquire salvation through a "vicarious baptism of desire"—that is, through the desire of their parents, the Church, or someone else. Along these lines, it is a common practice within the post-abortion healing movement to encourage mothers and fathers of aborted children to offer a solemn prayer in which they entrust their children to the care of Jesus. This is an important part of the healing experience for many women and men. There have also been reports of mystical experiences in which the dedication of the aborted child was prompted by an interior voice of the Holy Spirit,[5] and others who have prayerfully dedicated an aborted child to God have reported remarkable healing for the post-aborted mother and father or relatives who were not even aware that the prayer was made.[6]

Another theory, which was once widely taught in Catholic parochial schools, is that of Limbo. Contrary to popular belief, this theory has never been a dogma of the Catholic Church. It has always been nothing more than a theological speculation which offers one possible solution to the puzzle of God's judgment of unbaptized innocents.

According to the Limbo theory, God's justice precludes punishment of the innocent, but the requirement of baptism precludes the unbaptized from enjoying the actual presence of God, heaven. Given these two constraints, one can conclude that God must at least supply these souls with a place where they enjoy a state of natural happiness, free of all suffering, where they would lack only the beatific vision of God. This place would be analogous to the place where Abraham and Lazarus were at rest prior to the opening of heaven by Christ (Luke 16:22).

---

[5]Jack Hayford, *I'll Hold You in Heaven* (Ventura, CA: Regal Books, 1990), 47.

[6]Dr. Kenneth McAll, *Healing the Family Tree* (London: Sheldon Press, 1986), 27, 33, 34, 48, 52. McAll, a Protestant who was initially resistant to "prayers for the dead," provides a good discussion on the practices of the early Church regarding prayerful committal of the dead and how these accord with Scripture. See pages 88-97.

While Catholics are free to believe in Limbo, the official
Catechism encourages believers to hope for more, trusting that
God has another means for admitting unbaptized innocents into
heaven.[7] Indeed, the teaching documents of the Catholic Church
exclude any theory which would hold that salvation of unbaptized innocents is not possible.[8] Most recently, in fact, Pope John
Paul II has written in a major encyclical on abortion that *"nothing
is definitively lost* and you [the women and men who have pro-
cured abortions] will also be able to ask forgiveness from your
child, *who is now living in the Lord."*[9] [Italics added.] In short, while
the Catholic Church does not teach the salvation of aborted children as a dogmatic certainty, it strongly encourages us to hope for
their salvation through trust in God's mercy.

THE HOLY INNOCENTS

Nancyjo Mann, the founder of Women Exploited by Abortion,
once suggested that the slaughter of infants has always preceded
the coming of a savior. Infant boys were slaughtered by Pharaoh
before the coming of Moses. The infants of Bethlehem were
slaughtered by Herod, who sought to prevent the Messiah from
gaining his throne. Perhaps, she speculated, the slaughter of millions of babies by abortion throughout the world is a precursor to
Christ's return.

No one knows when the Second Coming will be (Mark 13:32).
Indeed, the moment we begin to feel certain that we do know is
the moment we almost certainly prove that we are wrong (Mark
13:33). Throughout the ages, Christians have looked at the

---

[7] Catechism of the Catholic Church, 1261.

[8] Vatican II documents, reflecting on God's saving will, include the dogmatic statement that "since Christ died for all (Rom. 8:32)...we must hold that the Holy
Spirit offers to all the possibility of being made partners, in a way known to God,
in the paschal mystery" (*Gaudium et Spes*, 22). This statement would seem to
weigh against the theory of Limbo. If an unborn child is denied the opportunity
of baptism by water, then "the possibility of being made partners" in Christ's
redemption must mean that some other means of sanctification is available.

[9] John Paul II, *Evangelium Vitae* (The Gospel of Life), 99.

world's sinfulness and said, "Certainly He will come to judge us now." Our age is no different. Few Christians would doubt that the horrors of our generation demand judgment. But while we should all pray for Christ's return tomorrow, we must never neglect our task of building up His kingdom today.

It is true. This sinful age, with its own slaughter of innocents, will not be allowed to go on forever. God will not be mocked. So there are only three possibilities: (1) Christ will return; or (2) God, who is the Lord of History, will crush our modern civilization, adding its dust to the ruins of all the other proud empires which have gone before us; or (3) to glorify God's own Mercy, the Holy Spirit will conquer our love affair with death by bringing about a time of awakening, healing, and spiritual renewal. I do not know which of these God has ordained, His return, our culture's destruction, or our culture's spiritual healing. I do know that we, His followers, can only contribute to the latter. This is our task now, as it was from the beginning, to spread the good news of God's mercy and forgiveness.

But I have strayed a bit. My real reason for bringing up the Holy Innocents who were slaughtered by Herod is that they have been traditionally considered as assured of heavenly repose by virtue of the fact that they died in an attack on Christ. This was a form of martyrdom. They did not die in defense of their faith, for they did not know it, but rather as victims of mass murder directed against the Messiah.

If we believe the Holy Innocents are in Heaven, then this belief, too, should encourage us to believe in the salvation of the unborn who die by abortion. For whether Christ's return is imminent or not, abortion in our culture is clearly the result of a diabolical attack on Christian values. In the larger scheme of things, it is an attempt by Satan to usurp the Lord of Life and install a cult of death. It is an attack against the Body of Christ, His Church, which includes the vast majority of aborting women and men, who belong to the Church by virtue of their own baptisms. In this attack on Christ's body, unborn children are the innocent casualties. It is therefore reasonable to assume that, like the Holy Innocents, they too are baptized in their own blood, and, in this way, will be brought into a share of Christ's own bloody baptism.

Summary

We must be confident of God's mercy, not only toward us, but also toward the unborn. If God has mercy on anyone, certainly He will be merciful with them.

Those who seek post-abortion healing must recognize that fears about the salvation of their unborn children are a temptation toward despair—a temptation which must be resisted. If they desire to be reunited with their aborted children, they must not worry about the salvation of their children, but rather about their own salvation, to which end they must build up lives of faith, *hope*, and charity. Of these, the virtue of hope precludes doubts about whether God will have mercy on the unborn.

For those who seek an end to abortion, confidence in God's mercy toward the children killed by abortion should undergird efforts to minister to those who have lost their children to abortion. By helping them to find spiritual healing, we will be helping them to become instruments of God's will. As His instruments, it is they, speaking with the wisdom of their own experiences, who will bring an end to abortion. We must remember that this is their battle even more than ours. By helping them, we help the cause of respect for all human life.

CHAPTER FIVE

SAMPLES OF THE JERICHO SERMONS IN THREE STEPS

THE following three sermons are intended as an example of a series of sermons which build upon each other to cover all seven steps of the Jericho Plan as previously outlined in the introduction. Because some people may not hear all three sermons, each sermon is also designed to stand on its own, at least in the sense of achieving two principal objectives: (1) establishing at the very beginning an attitude of understanding, compassion, and non-judgmentalism toward those who have been involved in abortion; and (2) in all cases building up hope that those who have been involved in abortion can be released from any shame or guilt which continues to hold them bound to their secret.

These sermons are meant only as examples of what can be done. Additional issues, topics, quotes, testimonies, and topic "bits" suitable for formulating your own sermons are provided in the following chapters.

SERMON ONE

Goal

1. Increasing the congregation's empathy and compassion for post-aborted women.
2. Reducing the defensiveness of those involved in abortion and stimulating their desire to be understood.

Strategy Outline

1. Approach the topic of abortion slowly so that by the time your

listeners know what you are talking about, they already know that you are not seeking to condemn them.

2. Build first on our general duty to avoid judging others, while maintaining the rightness of judging the objective moral content of specific acts.

3. Clarify the distinction between objective evil and subjective culpability.

4. Build a basis for understanding the many pressures women face which make abortion appear to be their "only choice."

5. Share a testimony so that everyone can empathize with why women feel pressured into abortion and how deeply they can suffer from it afterwards.

6. Preview some of the emotional baggage carried by those who have been involved in abortion and suffered its detrimental effects on their lives.

7. Close with an appeal for compassion and understanding so that, as a community, we can help to alleviate the powerful sense of shame which obstructs repentance and healing.

JUDGE NOT, LEST YE BE JUDGED

"Judge not, lest ye be judged." How often have we heard that warning? Yet it is such an easy one to forget, especially when another person's sins seem to be so grievously wrong, so *obviously* wrong. Sometimes we can't help but ask ourselves, "How could anyone do such a thing?"

It's so easy to think that the sins of others are the result of a terrible selfishness, callousness, moral bankruptcy, or some deep flaw in their character. But if the truth were known, under the right circumstances, the right pressures, the right fears, we are all weak and susceptible to sin—even the gravest of sins.

"There but for the grace of God go I." This is how we must look on those who committed sins which we abhor. We must look on them not with an air of superiority or condemnation, but with an attitude of *humble* sympathy, empathy, and compassion, being thankful to God that we have been spared their great trials and falls. In humility we must all remember that without the grace of

God, each one of us is capable of *any* sin. If we have been spared knowing this sin or that, it is the grace of God alone which has protected us, not any virtuous excellence of our own character. We are all flawed. We all make bad judgments. We all make decisions in haste, ignorance, and confusion. We all have made bad decisions based not on moral reflection, but on the basis of emotions such as fear and despair.

Another reason we should not judge others is that we are in no position to judge their culpability, their personal responsibility for a sin. For example, stealing a man's wallet is a grave sin which always offends God—that is, it is never approved by God. But if a young child, such as Dickens's Oliver Twist, is told by a trusted adult, Fagan in this example, that taking the wallet of a merchant is a "game," the child's culpability is lessened, or even eliminated, by ignorance, or even uncertainty, about what is right or wrong. Or if, instead of being ignorant, Oliver had been threatened with injury to himself or a loved one unless he stole the merchant's wallet, that, too, would lessen or even eliminate his guilt because then his decision to steal was not truly a free choice. In either case, the act of stealing is objectively sinful. Let us make no mistake about that. Stealing, under any circumstance, offends God. But because God understands when our choices to sin are the result of coercive pressures, confusion, or ignorance, He may not hold us fully responsible for the consequence of our actions.

In this way, God is like any good father or mother who knows that we must judge the behavior of our children with both firmness and compassion. Parents know that it is important to always disapprove of acts which are objectively wrong, yet, at the same time, they understand that their children may not always be fully responsible for their actions. This knowledge tempers both their judgment and punishment of their children.

Another way of looking at this is to remember that we should always condemn acts which are morally wrong, but we should never condemn the persons who commit these acts because we can never know what was in their minds or hearts that may have lessened their culpability.

To live our lives in defense of the truth, we must be able and willing to judge the morality of *acts*. But the judgment of *individuals* must always be left to God. He alone knows the hearts and minds of us all. He alone knows how to judge how culpable we are for any of our actions. The old saying that we should "hate the sin, but love the sinner" is intended to remind us that we must be compassionate and understanding. Indeed, out of humility and generosity, we should always assume, and pray, that the sins of others are mitigated by some sort of ignorance or lack of freedom which will lessen their culpability in the eyes of God.

This reminder that we should not judge others is especially important with regard to the issue of abortion. It is extremely unfortunate that at least a few pro-lifers have become so preoccupied by the horrible reality of abortion that they immediately assume that those who have abortions are horrible people. It's simply not true. It is even extremely unfair. The women and men who choose abortion are often acting out of ignorance or fear, or under tremendous pressures.

Indeed, studies show that 70 percent of the women choosing abortion believe it is morally wrong. This fact alone tells us that women are choosing abortion not because they think it is the *right* thing to do, but because they think, due to whatever pressures they are facing, that it is the *only* thing they can do. They feel trapped. Consider, for example, this testimony from an eighteen-year-old girl whom we will call Tracy:

> My family would not support my decision to keep my baby. My boyfriend said he would give me no emotional or financial help whatsoever. All the people who mattered to me told me to abort. When I said I didn't want to, they started listing all the reasons why I should. They said it would be detrimental to my career, and my health, and that I would have no social life and no future with men. Could I actually do it alone? *I started feeling like maybe I was crazy to want to keep it.*
>
> I finally just told everyone that I would have the abortion just to get them off my back. But inside, I still didn't want to have the abortion. Unfortunately, when the abortion day came, I shut off my inside feelings. I was scared to not do it because of how my family and boyfriend felt. I'm so angry at myself for giving in to the pressure of others. I just felt *so alone* in my feelings to have my baby.

Was Tracy responsible for her decision to have an abortion? Yes. But was she *fully* culpable for that decision? No. She was faced with tremendous pressures and confusion. In her story we see that Tracy had no support to help her do what her heart told her was right. Instead, she was being "socially aborted"; she was being cut off from all of the social support she needed and expected from her family, friends, and boyfriend. She was being made to choose between her love for her baby and her love for everyone else in her life. What a terrible choice! What an unfair choice. But it is a choice that thousands of women face every day.

Researchers have found that well over half of the women who are choosing abortions would have been willing to carry their children to term if they had received support to do so by the important people in their lives. But without this support, or indeed when faced with threats that they will lose their loved ones, it is very hard to resist the temptation to give in to abortion. One woman who made this decision has commented that she "made the decision to be weak." She didn't decide to have an abortion so much as she decided not to resist all the pressures which were pushing her toward the abortion. For years she lived with the pain of a great self-hatred. She hated herself for being weak—too weak to stand up for her beliefs, too weak to stand up for her child.

We also know from the testimonies of women who have had abortions, and dozens of former abortionists like Dr. Bernard Nathanson and Carol Everett, that there is a tremendous amount of deceit and manipulation which goes on in abortion clinics. Women are not only denied the truth about their unborn children and about the damage abortion will cause to their lives, they are also carefully maneuvered into believing that abortion is their *only* choice. After all, abortion clinics are operated to maximize profit. So-called abortion counselors are really specialists at only one thing: selling abortion. They treat abortion like a cure-all for every unplanned pregnancy. If a young woman admits, "I would really like to have this baby," the counselor is trained to identify her fears and anxieties and then push all the right buttons to convince her that the idea of having her baby is just a romantic dream. "Where will you get $6,000 to pay the hospital bills?" they ask. "How will you ever pay for food or diapers? You've already hurt your parents once, don't make it worse. Don't make yourself into a burden on everyone. Besides, you're not ready to be a parent, and who will be the one to suffer from your mistakes? Your baby."

Yes. Abortion counselors are trained to make women feel guilty about *not* having an abortion. Every day, young girls are being made to feel that they are doing their unborn babies a favor by having an abortion. Some are even told that their desire to keep their baby is "selfish"; they are told that that only by submitting to an abortion will they be acting with maturity and taking "responsibility" for their lives.

In today's society, the pressures to abort are so great that all of us should truly admire the young single women who are strong enough to stand up against those who want them to abort and say "No." It's not easy to take such a stand. It's not easy to face the judgments of others. It's not easy to be a single mother, and it's not easy to give a child you love into the hands of adopting parents. We really need to admire the courage of these young women. And on the other hand, we really need to refrain from judging those whose courage failed them. Haven't we, too, lost our courage at times, especially at the worst of times?

We must also have the greatest of empathy and compassion for those who have chosen abortion, or been involved in abortions in any more distant way, because the impact of abortion on a person's life can be truly devastating. These women and men must live with the memory of a child they have never been able to hold. They suffer from feelings of self-doubt, lowered self-esteem, and grief. They may be their own most fierce condemners, often doubting even God's ability to forgive them. The emotional pain of those who have had abortions can be extremely intense, and it can cause all kinds of disruptions in a person's life.

In our example of Tracy, her negative reaction began immediately after her abortion. In this, her case is actually unusual, since most women don't begin to confront their post-abortion feelings for an average of five years or more after their abortion. Most women are able to push down their negative feelings, hide them, or deny them for quite a long time. But in Tracy's case, she immediately experienced a tremendous amount of self-loathing. To her, there was never any doubt that what she had aborted was her child, a child she wanted. She simply couldn't see how she could live with herself after what she had done. So two days after her abortion, Tracy took her father's gun out of its case and held it to her mouth to commit suicide. Fortunately, she heard her father come home for lunch, and she couldn't bring herself to pull the trigger while he was in the house. So instead, she went upstairs and had lunch with him, and by the time he left, she was trembling with so much fear she couldn't go through with it. It was then that she came upon the idea of trying to make up for the abortion by tricking her boyfriend into making her pregnant again.

This desire for replacement pregnancies to make up for an abortion is very common. Approximately one in three women who have had an abortion try to become pregnant again specifically to replace the child they lost in their abortion. About 18 percent of women who abort actually become pregnant within one year of their abortion. But many times, they face the same pressures to abort that they did the first time, and so many end up having another abortion, or even a third or a fourth. For some women, repeat abortions can become a form of self-punishment. Each time they abort, they are hurting themselves and trying to harden themselves to the pain of the first. For other women, repeat pregnancies and repeat abortions are like a reenactment of what they suffered before. Each time, they hope on some level to break free of the cycle, and sometimes they do, but sometimes they don't. So we must understand that, when women have more than one abortion, it does not mean that they were not bothered by their first abortion. It probably means exactly the opposite. It means that their first abortion has left them so psychologically disturbed that they can't help but get into situations where they face another abortion decision. So even when a woman has had more than one abortion, we must not judge her. We must not make assumptions about her culpability for what she has done. God alone can judge her guilt.

In our dealings with those who have been involved in abortion—whether in one or thousands of abortions, as in the case of an abortion provider—we need to be generous in offering them our sympathy, understanding, and charity. We must do this because all of them, on one level or another, have been deeply bruised and battered by their abortions. By judging them harshly, we are putting up walls between them and the Church; we are driving them away from the God of Judgment instead of toward the God of Forgiveness.

If we truly desire to transform the world, then we must begin by replacing judgmentalism with charity. We must work to relieve these women and men of the shame which makes them afraid to seek reconciliation in Christ. We must be people who can listen to the words "I've had an abortion" and react, not with horror, but with compassion. To do this, we must first transform our own hearts. We must fully understand that the choice to abort is one which is filled with great doubts and pain, and those who make it are driven by fears and confusion which will maintain a hold on them for years, decades, or even a lifetime. Instead of condemnation, we need always and everywhere to offer hope to all those who have ever been involved in an abortion. We must offer them the hope that we will be understanding, not condemning. And even more importantly, we need to lead and support them in the hope that, by turning themselves over to the loving mercy of God, they can and will be fully healed and even transformed into the champions of life that God wants them to be.

SERMON TWO

Goals

3. Educating the congregation about the many symptoms of post-abortion trauma, including its destructive effects on the lives of women, men, and families.
4. Explaining how and why denial and avoidance behaviors are obstacles to healing which prolong psychological and spiritual suffering.

Strategy Outline

1. Continue to ostensibly be "lecturing" those who have not had abortions. This choice of audience allows those who have had abortions to avoid feeling that they are the ones being "lectured to" yet still "listen in" and learn more their own post-abortion experience and how it is your goal, and that of your whole community, to help them.
2. Review and reinforce the need to have sympathy for those involved in abortion and the desire to promote healing and reconciliation.
3. Discuss how despair can be used to lead us into error and how it can also be used to keep us away from being reunited with God.
4. Describe some of the psychosocial problems caused by unresolved abortion guilt. This overview is important to help post-

aborted persons and their loved ones see how the problems in their lives may be related to a past abortion. In this way, they are helped to begin to break through the denial that "my abortion didn't affect me."

5. Discuss the emotional and spiritual importance of overcoming avoidance behavior and working through post-abortion issues. Note that this may be difficult to do at times, but that there is lots of help available, especially from people who have been through the very same experience.

6. End with reaffirmation of the community's support.

THE DEVIL'S BARGAIN

I've spoken to you before about the need to be compassionate and understanding toward the women, men, and families who have been involved in abortion. The temptation to judge them and condemn them is a great evil because such attitudes push people away from the embrace of God's healing. Such attitudes build up walls and drive people away. Instead, while never condoning abortion, we must recognize the great pressures which make people feel they have no choice but to abort, and we must recognize the great need they feel afterward to be fully reconciled with God, their community, and themselves.

When women and men are faced with an unplanned pregnancy, their lives are turned upside down. They may face tremendous pressures to abort from other people, from circumstances, or simply from within, because the birth of a child threatens the status quo. It threatens what they have and treasure here and now.

Many women are openly threatened by loved ones that if they keep the child, they will lose the love and support they need and desire from their boyfriend, husband, or even their parents. Or maybe they feel that their future career plans are threatened, or they fear losing the chance to have the type of home and family they have always planned. After all, the problem with unplanned pregnancies is that they throw off our plans. They make us feel out of control. And we all like to feel in control, don't we?

Now picture yourself like one of those cartoon characters who has an angel on one shoulder whispering advice into our ear and a devil on the other shoulder. You've just learned that you or a loved one, a spouse or a daughter, is pregnant. The news makes you feel trapped. All your plans for the future, for yourself, or for your loved one, now seem scattered to the wind. What should you do?

Your guardian angel whispers into your ear, "Trust God. What looks like a burden is actually a gift. You may not see how, but God has a plan for you and this child. The sacrifices you will have to make now will be rewarded a hundred-fold."

But the devil whispers instead, "Sure babies are good. But not now! You're not ready for it. It will ruin everything. Nothing will ever be the same again. You have to save what you have. An abortion will give you back control over your life. Then you can save what you have, save what you've been working for, save the love of the people for whom you and this baby will be just another burden. Make this little sacrifice now, give up this pregnancy and wait for another day, and you won't have to lose anything. You can save it all."

So it is that God asks us, in trusting Him, to risk everything on a future for which we have not planned, while Satan asks us to give up just one little thing, an unborn child, to keep control over our lives and save everything we have planned for. The devil uses despair, the fear of losing what we have, to make us do things which we would normally reject. No one likes abortion, but if we fear that we will lose more than we can bear, many of us will cave in and accept it as an "evil necessity."

But the devil's bargain is a false one. Abortion does not turn back the clock. It is not something a person can have and forget. After an abortion, *everything* is *still* changed. After the abortion, Satan, who used despair to drive the woman to choose abortion, now uses despair to destroy the woman in other ways. He becomes the woman's accuser. "You've killed your own child. You've always wanted children, but now you've gone and killed a child instead! You're a terrible person. You betrayed yourself and your child. God will never forgive you. He'll punish you. Sooner or later, He'll get you. And everyone else will despise you, too. So you had better keep this one a secret, especially from those goodie-two-shoes who don't know what it is like. They would only want you to suffer even more than you are already. So if you need a little comfort, you might as well find it in the embrace of an affair, the bottom of a bottle, or even in the silence of suicide. You did this to yourself, and now you are *alone* and you will have to live with it—*alone*."

So it is that Satan tries to use the same shame, fear, and despair which drive women to abort to keep them from finding the healing compassion of God and their communities. That is Satan's agenda. But what is Christ's? Does Christ desire punishment for those who have had abortions? No. He desires reconciliation. After an abortion, or any sin, Christ offers us hope. He stands with open arms greeting us, saying, "Come to me. I want to share your tears. I want to comfort you. Know that all is forgiven. See, your child is in my arms, waiting for you to join us when your day is completed."

This is the difference between Satan and Christ. Before we sin, Satan is "on our side," offering us excuses to defend our sin. After our sin, Satan is our condemner. Christ, on the other hand, stands before us with arms outstretched asking us not to go this sinful way. But afterwards, He, who has a right to condemn us, offers us forgiveness instead. But Satan does not want us to be reconciled with God. So he tempts us to fear God's judgment and to fear the judgment of people around us.

No matter what our sins may be, we must always resist the temptation to despair of God's forgiveness. It is true that we don't deserve God's forgiveness, but it is a gift which He wants us to have.

For those who have been involved in an abortion, their sin was that of refusing God's gift of life. To these people we must say, "Don't commit the sin of refusing this second gift, the gift of God's forgiveness, the rebirth of your spirit in Christ."

And we must all play a role in bringing the healing gift of God's mercy to others. As one woman who had an abortion has written, "It takes the blood of Jesus to deliver us from guilt, but it takes the acceptance of others to deliver us from shame." By this, she is telling us that the road to recovery from an abortion is not always simple and easy. Even after one accepts God's forgiveness, there is still the temptation to not forgive ourselves and to live in dread of the judgment of others. Such fears and doubts create obstacles to developing and maintaining open and loving relationships. They rob us of the joy in life which God wants for us.

This is why the emotional consequences of abortion are so severe. Women who have abortions are four times more likely to engage in drug or alcohol abuse. They are more likely to have dif-ficulty maintaining good relationships with men and to experience sexual dysfunctions. They have higher divorce rates, are more likely to seek psychological counseling, and are more likely to be less healthy physically. Approximately half of the women who have had an abortion experience suicidal thoughts, with over one in five actually reporting having attempted suicide. Many experience difficulty bonding with later children because they have not finished going through the necessary process of mourning the loss of their aborted children.

Others become obsessive mothers; they are overprotective because they feel a need to make up for their abortions or because they fear that since God is planning to punish them, He may do so by hurting their subsequent children. Some struggle every day with intrusive thoughts of their abortion, which can make it difficult for them to concentrate on their work or family. Others struggle to avoid thoughts of their abortion; they get all up-tight seeing articles about abortion in the newspaper; they hate the sound of vacuum cleaners because it reminds them of the suction aspirator; or they are bothered by the sight of little children who would be the same age as the child they lost during their own abortion. They may have unexplained feelings of depression every year, during the month when the abortion took place, or during the month when the child should have been born, or on Mother's Day or at Christmas.

In these and a hundred different ways, abortion can cast a pallor over a man or a woman's life. And in many cases, it can result in severe physical and emotional problems from which it can take years, or even decades, to recover. One study has found that, on average, it takes over eight years for a woman to even begin dealing with the emotional baggage of a past abortion. Most women simply suffer silently because they feel that no one will understand. After all, in our society, abortion is supposed to be something that "helps" women. Women's lives are, at least in theory, supposed to be improved by abortion. So most women endure their pains and doubts in silence, or they try to push them down and deny that they have those pains and doubts simply because they fear it would be too hard to confront them.

But by creating a healing environment, one which frees women and men from shame and fear of judgment, we can help them come more quickly to feel at peace with God, themselves, and our community. Only in this way will they eventually be free from the pain and temptation of despair. Only in this way will they recover the full joy and peace of mind which God desires for them.

But why, you may ask, don't we simply "let sleeping dogs lie". Why not just let memories of an abortion remain buried and forgotten? There are a lot of answers to this question, the most obvious being that, like the sleeping dog, these buried memories inevitably wake up. Worse yet, as long as these feelings and memories remain buried, they will continue to bubble up as an ongoing series of problems and disruptions in a person's life. They demand our notice precisely because we are trying to ignore them. In this way, buried memories are just like a neglected child; the more we ignore them, the more trouble they cause.

Perhaps most importantly, the failure to reconcile a history of abortion has spiritual consequences. Many women and men will try to run from their past by trying to *rationalize* their choice. They become fixated on trying to make arguments to convince themselves and others that the abortion was somehow excusable, or even for the best. The spiritual consequence of such rationalization is that it involves a denial of objective moral truth. It is a choice which leads one to live in darkness, in a dreamland of one's own creation, rather than in the light of Christ.

As long as one clings to rationalizations, one cannot truly cling to Christ. Which would you really rather have? The cold comfort of excuses or the warm embrace of our Heavenly Father, who not only forgives us, but kills the fatted calf to celebrate our return?

There are other women and men who don't try to excuse their mistakes; they know they did the wrong thing, but they simply try to push it out of their minds. To help them push down negative feelings and memories, they may become compulsively busy with work or hobbies because they simply can't stand any quiet time for reflection or contemplation. Some bury their regrets and pain in drug abuse or alcoholism. In all these cases, people are denying themselves the greatest fruits of life. They do not truly know peace and contentment because they are running from their past. Because they are avoiding contemplation, they also end up avoiding prayer, and in avoiding prayer, they are avoiding God, who is actually the only One who can free them from their past.

These things are true for all sins, not just abortion. When we try to rationalize or excuse our sins, we are actually holding ourselves back from the embrace of Christ's forgiveness. In addition, when we are afraid to confront and acknowledge our sins, it is then that we are most entrapped by them.

The solution is found in humbly and courageously facing our sinful past. We must let go of our excuses. With a humility born in the knowledge that God truly loves us, we must open our eyes to the truth. We are His children, and He so desires to make us whole—in Him alone—that He will forgive us anything. Indeed, He came to die for us, accepting the punishment we deserve for our sins, so that we would be free from the shackles of sin which hold us to the past. Instead of hiding from our past sins, we must confront them squarely and give them over to Christ. Sometimes the shame or pain is so great that it is not easy to do. But with prayer, *and the help of each other*, it can always be done.

SERMON THREE

Goals

5. Building up confidence in the post-aborted that they will be understood, accepted, and supported by their community.

6. Stimulating the desire for emotional and spiritual healing.

7. Encouraging reconciliation with God through acknowledgment of one's personal responsibility for the abortion(s), and inviting participation in post-abortion recovery programs.

Strategy Outline

1. Build up hope in the truth that God can resurrect good from any evil.

2. Build up confidence that aborted children enjoy the eternal happiness of heaven.

3. Build up faith that even our sins can be used by God to make us into better people.

4. Develop the understanding that the only lasting victims of abortion are those who fail to embrace God's forgiveness.

5. Paint a picture of the joy of healing which has been experienced by so many women and men who have worked through post-abortion healing.

6. Invite the members of your community to help each other and those who have been involved in abortion to participate in post-abortion healing.

MIRACLES NEVER END

The Resurrection! It is the miracle *par excellence*. It is filled with more meaning than we can ever fully contemplate. It is not just the miracle of Jesus coming back to life. Others have been raised from the dead: the widow's son, who was raised by the prayers of Elijah; Lazarus and the daughter of the synagogue leader, who were raised by Jesus; and Tabitha, who was raised by the prayers of Peter. But the meaning of their resurrections was confined to a display of God's power and love. The resurrection of Christ was a display of God's *forgiveness*.

Unlike the other biblical characters who died from disease and were raised back to life, Jesus died after being tortured and executed. In the person of Jesus, God handed *Himself* over to be killed by sinners who represent all the sinners of history, including us. He died because of *our* sins. We are responsible for His death.

Imagine the guilt you would feel if you ran down an innocent pedestrian with your car. Perhaps you were selfishly speeding. Perhaps you were unthinkingly drunk. Perhaps you had been in a fit of rage and simply did it out of a crazed fury. But as soon as you did it, the guilt began to fill your belly with regret, fear and panic.

What are you to do? You are guilty! You deserve to be punished—but you're *afraid* of being punished. So you run away. You hide the truth from others and yourself. But no matter how far you run, or how you try to push it out of your mind, you will never be able to forget that terrible sound and that bump of the car as you drove over your victim. That, my dear friends, that is guilt.

But now imagine that one day a person comes to your door. It is the same person you killed, but now he is alive. He was truly dead, but through a miracle of God, now he is alive! And not just alive, but alive with a heavenly splendor which is so beautiful and majestic it is almost terrifying. Why, you wonder, has he come to you, his killer? Has he come for vengeance? For retribution? You know you deserve whatever penalty he might demand of you. But no. Your victim has not come to condemn you, but instead to offer you forgiveness. His only desire is to free you of the guilt which has haunted you for all these years. All you have to do is to believe and accept this truth, and your guilt is gone. You will be saved not by your virtue, but by your victim's *immortality*. He is not dead. He is alive, and your guilt is gone *because* he lives.

In just the same way we have all been forgiven of murder. Because by our sins, of whatever type, each of us is guilty of crucifying Christ. Because of our sins, He was killed. His blood is on our hands. Yet on Easter Sunday, He rose from the dead. He is not dead at all! The guilt has been lifted.

In the Resurrection, God shows not only his mercy, but also His unbounded ability to turn tragedy into triumph. From any defeat, He can draw out a victory. From any sin which brings death to the soul, He can bring forth sorrow, renewal, and a rebirth into a glorious life which was unthinkable before.

In the Resurrection we learn that the experience of sin need not conquer us; instead, Christ can use it to bring us back to Him with greater love than we have ever known before. In acknowledging our sin, we find humility. And in humility, we find Mercy—for Jesus is Mercy incarnate. And in accepting Mercy, we experience the unconditional love of God which will transform our lives forever.

But the miracle of the Resurrection is not limited to our relationship with God. This miracle also extends to our relationship with each other. In the Resurrection, we learn that death is an experience, not the end our being. For "God is not the God of the dead but of the living. All are alive for Him." (Luke 20:38.)

C.S. Lewis explains it well when he writes, "There are no ordinary people. You have never talked to a mere mortal. Nations, cultures, arts, civilization—these are mortal, and their life is to ours as the life of a gnat. But it is immortals whom we joke with, work with, marry, snub and exploit—immortal horrors or everlasting splendors." Damned or glorified all people live on. (Matt. 25:46.)

And what of the innocent children who are killed by abortion? They, too, are alive in Christ! Jesus himself assures us that it is our heavenly Father's plan that not a single one of these little ones shall ever be lost. (Luke 18:14.) They are immortal souls. And because they live in Christ, they live with hearts of mercy. They sit in Christ's lap, praying for an end to abortion, for the forgiveness of their parents and those who have assisted in or provided abortions.

They pray not for vengeance, but for forgiveness, so that their parents will be washed clean of guilt and united with them, their children, in Christ.

Pope John Paul II has echoed this same message in speaking especially to the women who have had abortions. He says, "Do not give in to discouragement and do not lose hope. Try rather to understand what happened and face it honestly. If you have not already done so, give yourselves over with humility and trust to repentance. The Father of mercies is ready to give you his forgiveness and peace in the Sacrament of Reconciliation. You will come to understand that *nothing* is definitively lost and you will also be able to ask forgiveness from your child, *who is now living in the Lord*." Listen to what the Pope is saying. "Nothing is definitively lost." Everything can be restored. Why? Because your child is now "living in the Lord." It is the miracle of the Resurrection. It is the hit-and-run victim at the door saying: "You do not have to be afraid anymore. You do not have to hide the truth any longer. For I am alive. You are forgiven. Go forth with joy and sin no more."

Do you realize that it is one of the great mysteries of God's grace that He can use our sins to make better people out of us? I don't mean that He ever wants us to sin, but when we do, He can use our sins to teach us of our need to rely on Him. He can teach us humility.

I truly believe that there are no souls among us who have greater humility, or greater compassion for the failings of others, than the women and men who have had abortions, acknowledged their sins, and discovered the wonder of God's healing compassion. Ask Paul, the persecutor of the Christians on the way to Damascus. Only those who have sinned greatly, only those with the blood of innocents on their hands, can fully experience the unlimited glory of God's forgiveness. Is there no limit to His love, that we can be forgiven even the killing of our own children? Only those who have experienced such forgiveness can fully appreciate what I am talking about. It is life-transforming. It is the miraculous lifting of a great and terrible weight. It is not just being born again, it is the witnessing of a miracle. It is a *participation* in the Resurrection of Christ.

This is the experience which has been shared by many women and men who have carried the guilt of an abortion with them for years, or even decades. They have found that when they stop making excuses for their abortions, and instead confess them and trust in God's loving care for their children—who are really our Heavenly Father's children—they are made free, and clean, and whole.

It does not always happen in just a moment, because Satan tries to use the memory of our sins to hold us back. Even after we accept Christ's forgiveness, Satan will try to use doubt, fear, and despair to deny us the full experience of healing which God wants for us. But if you have ever had an abortion, or you know of someone else who has, you must take heart in knowing that there are other people who have already been down this road. They want to help you. They can help you. They understand everything you have been through because they have been there too. The first step is prayer. The second step is trusting in others to help you along the way.

I invite any of you who want to help the women and men in our congregation along the path of post-abortion healing to contact me about how you can help to build an effective outreach and healing effort in our community. I also want to invite any of you who have had or have been involved in abortions and are still troubled by it in any way, to come speak with me in private, or to participate in post-abortion healing programs offered in our area, or to call a counselor at one of the national hotlines listed in the bulletin.

Finally, I would ask everyone to pray for the people in our congregation, our city, and our nation who continue to struggle with the guilt of abortion. Bow your heads now, and let us join together in prayer for all those who have completed, are travelling, or are about to begin, the wonderful, but sometimes scary and difficult journey to the joy of a complete post-abortion healing. (*Lead the congregation in spontaneous prayer or in the Lord's Prayer.*)

CHAPTER SIX

MISCELLANY

THIS chapter contains material suitable for publication in your weekly bulletin, "bits and pieces" for your sermons, and an assortment of thoughts which will help you to gain further insights into the needs of women and men in your community who are scarred by abortion.

AFTER AN ABORTION: STEPS TOWARD HEALING

1. Recognize that the road to full recovery can take time and effort. God's forgiveness can be had instantly, but sorting out your life and your feelings, overcoming the ever-present temptation to give in again to despair and doubt—these take time.

2. Recognize that it is normal and good to mourn the loss of a loved one. Just as mourning the loss of a parent or spouse takes time, so does mourning the loss of an aborted child. In the case of abortion, the mourning process is often cut short and never completed because of denial or feelings of guilt which block the mourning process. You must courageously allow the mourning process to get back on track. Accept your grief as normal rather than something which must covered up or pushed away. Recognize that the pain of your loss will fade as your healing progresses.

3. Recognize that you are not alone. Others have been through the same experience and the same trials. Their experiences and understanding can help you. They *want* to help you, just as you may want to help others after you have finished going through the healing process.

4. Admit your personal responsibility but also recognize that others, too, were involved. Pray for God's forgiveness for both yourself

and everyone else who either encouraged the abortion or failed to help you avoid the abortion.

5. Forgive yourself. God does not want you to live a lifetime in mourning. Your sin has been forgiven. You have been made new in Christ. Rejoice in the knowledge that one day you will be with your child in the arms of the Lord.

6. Forgive others. Recognize that they, too, acted out of ignorance, fear, or petty human selfishness. If possible, let them know that you forgive them. Forgive even the abortion providers.

7. Give your childen over to the care of God, their Heavenly Father, and the true Parent of us all. Know that they are loved, happy, and well cared for. They, too, desire your joy and happiness. They miss you, but they do not resent or condemn you, because they live in the love and mercy of Christ. Do not try to hold onto them by prolonging your grief; hold onto them by sharing their happiness in heaven.

THE DECISION TO FORGIVE

Husbands, what would you do if your wife were to turn to you one night and tell you of her pain over a past abortion? What if it was her deepest secret? Could you embrace her and support her without judgment? Could you open yourself to hearing everything she wants to tell? Or would you cut her off short, even with words of kindness, because it makes you too uncomfortable to hear all that she feels, all that she has experienced? Would your love for her be deepened by her willingness to share her greatest secret with you?

I could also ask the same thing of you wives. How would you respond to your husband's admission that he had been involved in a past abortion? Or what if an abortion decision was *jointly* made by both of you? If you have been able to forget about it, but your spouse has secretly carried a heavy burden in silence, would you be willing to listen to the other's pain even if it meant allowing your own sense of peace to be disturbed? Or maybe both of you are carrying about an unspoken grief but neither has felt free to admit it. Whatever your motives for concealing your pain and

PLEASE return this Pastors Survey. We also invite you to send additional comments and suggestions.

	Strongly Disagree				Strongly Agree
The message in this book is one my congregation needs to hear.	1	2	3	4	5
This book will make it easier for me to preach on the abortion issue.	1	2	3	4	5
I definitely plan on using material from this book.	1	2	3	4	5
With this approach I plan to speak more frequently on abortion and post-abortion healing.	1	2	3	4	5
I would be interested in receiving a free newsletter for pastors expanding on the contents of this book.	1	2	3	4	5
I would be interested in contributing insights or sermon material to such a newsletter.	1	2	3	4	5

Name: _____

Address: _____

_____

City: _____ State: ___ Zip: _____ Phone: _____
(optional)

See what our readers are saying about *The Post-Abortion Review.*

"Your newsletter is TOP-NOTCH! God bless you for your hard work."

"I'm so excited about your new publication! I've gone through an abortion myself, just two years ago. This is a much needed area of research."

"Incredibly powerful! If only more people would read it, abortion would END!"

"Once in a while I read something that really makes me feel great, and this just happened to me. The whole newsletter is terrific."

Here are some of the titles you have already missed:

- **Abortion and the Feminization of Poverty**
- **Rape, Incest and Abortion: Searching Beyond the Myths**
- **New Study Confirms Link between Abortion and Substance Abuse**
- **Identifying High Risk Abortion Patients**
- **Abortion and Domestic Violence**

Elliot Institute
P.O. Box 7348
Springfield, IL 62791-7348

Please send me the following materials:

Qty		*Price*
____	*The Post-Abortion Review* (One year / 4 issues)	$20 donation
____	*Making Abortion Rare:* *A Healing Strategy for a Divided Nation*	$15 + s/h
____	*Aborted Women: Silent No More*	$16 + s/h
____	*The Jericho Plan: Breaking Down the Walls* *Which Prevent Post-Abortion Healing*	$ 9 + s/h

Shipping and handling (s/h): $3.50 for the first book, $1 for each additional book

Special Offer: Enclosed is a donation of $30, or more. Please send me a copy of *Making Abortion Rare* ($15 value) along with my first of four issues of *The Post-Abortion Review*. (No s/h fee with this offer.) **Check here:** ❑

Name: _____

Address: _____

_____

City: _____ State: ___ Zip: _____ Phone: _____
                                                              (optional)

Mail to: Elliot Institute, P.O. Box 7348-B, Springfield, IL 62781-7348
(Only want books? For faster service, call: **1-800-BOOKLOG** [800-266-5564])

Ask about our generous bulk discount rates, especially for *The Jericho Plan*.

burying your past, know that this kind of denial is an obstacle to true intimacy. It will be and will remain a hidden source of conflict, pain, and resentment throughout all aspects of your marriage—emotional, physical, and spiritual.

These are issues which are confronting many couples in this congregation, though often one member of the couple isn't even aware of the past abortion. But can you imagine how hard it would be for your spouse to share this secret with you if he or she is uncertain of your reaction?

So we must ask ourselves: How compassionate can we be? How forgiving? This is an important question which we should dwell on so that we can make the *decision* to be forgiving before the need to be forgiving arises.

Just to test ourselves further, imagine that your spouse were to confess tonight that ten years ago he or she had an abortion to cover up an extra-marital affair. How forgiving and understanding would you be then? Or what if the affair and abortion had occured only last year? Could you decide now, with the grace of God, that you would be forgiving and compassionate? I truly believe, and pray, that you could. And what if your spouse were to admit that she was pregnant right now as the result of some mindless fling last month? Could you make the decision, right now, with the grace of God, that you would continue to love her and the child unconditionally?

This, ladies and gentlemen, is the type of understanding, love, and forgiveness which is needed to create a pro-life society. The decision you can make today, to be understanding, compassionate, and forgiving will shape your emotions and reactions in the future. Your decision today can make you an ambassador of Christ's healing powers to the millions of women, men, grandparents, children, and siblings who are carrying about with them the pain of abortion, or any other shame. By our *decision* to be understanding, we help to lift others from the sorrow of shame to the joy of hope.

But *first* we must make the decision that this is the way we want to be. This is what is right. This is what is good.

Then, after making this decision, pray, and pray hard, that if you are ever told by any loved one of a past abortion, you will indeed be an instrument of healing and forgiveness. Pray that you will not let your own pride or self-righteousness create an obstacle to the healing and reconciliation of another with yourself and with God. When another person confesses his sins to you, you are being called upon to be an ambassador of Christ.

Remember too, that if you are struggling with an inability to forgive others, you simply MUST work your way through it with God's help. Pray for the ability to forgive. To not forgive is to injure yourself as much, or even more, than the one whom you are refusing to forgive.

An unforgiving attitude is an obstacle to our own happiness. Most importantly, it is an obstacle to salvation. Every time we pray "forgive us our trespasses AS we forgive those who trespass against us," we are entering into a covenant with God. We will be judged either liberally or stringently according to our own measure for forgiving others. If we carry about resentments against others, God will judge us with resentment. If we forgive others freely, God will forgive us freely. As Jesus himself clearly warns us, "If you do not forgive others, neither will your Father forgive you." (Matt. 6:15, 18:35)

I am not saying that forgiveness is always easy. Sometimes it is hard, very hard. But I am saying that forgiveness is always possible, and always necessary. Turn to God in prayer and ask for His help in forgiving others and in developing a forgiving attitude. Let us look for our example to Christ on the cross, who even while he was in the midst of his passion cried out words of forgiveness: "Father, forgive them, they know not what they do." So in the example of Jesus, we see that even when *we* are hurting, we can and must forgive others. And part of this ability to forgive others comes from knowing that more often than not, "they know not what they are doing."

People make bad decisions for all kinds of reasons. We all know that from personal experience. These bad decisions are bound up with the pressures of the moment, ignorance, emotions that have overcome our reason, or reason which is polluted by our own twisted selfishness. Forgive, then, not because our failures "don't matter," but because they matter so much that we *need each other* to recover from the pain caused by our mistakes.

So it is that we see two sides of the same coin: "Judge not, lest you be judged" and "Forgive each other as the Lord has forgiven you."

BITS AND PIECES

When the people brought the woman caught in adultery to Jesus, he said, let the one who has not sinned be the first to throw a stone. After they departed, he spoke to the woman: "Did none of them condemn you? Then neither do I condemn you. Go and sin no more." See what this story is showing us. Christ's mercy is manifested only AFTER the community, mindful of its own sinfulness, has withheld condemnation. In other words, by not condemning the sinner, we are making it possible, and even easier, for the sinner to be reconciled with Christ; by refusing to condemn others, we free the sinner to seek the mercy of God.

We are saved not by our merits, but by the wondrous mercy of God. Our salvation is not to our credit, but glorifies God, who can save "a wretch like me." Do not resist His forgiveness. Do not persist in your belief that you are unforgivable. You owe it to yourself, to your child, and to God, to allow Christ's glory to be manifested through His forgiveness of you, through His reform of your life.

The sin of abortion is the sin of refusing the miracle of God's gift of life. Don't commit the sin of refusing God's offer of a second miracle. It is the gift of God's forgiveness, the rebirth of your spirit in Christ.

ESPECIALLY RELEVANT BIBLE VERSES

"I am He who blots out your transgressions for My own sake and remembers your sin no more." Is. 43:25.

"No matter how deep the stain of your sins, I can take it out and make you as clean as freshly fallen snow....I can make you as white as wool." Adapted from Is. 1:18.

"If we confess our sins, He is faithful and just and will forgive us our sins and purify us from all unrighteousness." 1 John 1:9.

"When I kept silent, my bones wasted away through my groaning all day long, for day and night your hand was heavy upon me; my strength was sapped as in the heat of summer. Then I acknowledged my sin to you and did not cover my iniquity... and you forgave the guilt of my sin." Psalm 32:3-5. [Reflect on the great emotional burden involved in supporting the weight of denial and self-justification.]

"Rachel mourns her children, she refuses to be consoled because her children are no more. Thus says the Lord: Cease your cries of mourning. Wipe the tears from your eyes. The sorrow you have shown shall have its reward. There is hope for your future." Adapted from Jeremiah 31:15-17.

CATHOLIC POINTS

From *Evangelium Vitae* (The Gospel of Life), an encyclical letter of Pope John Paul II, March 25, 1995, paragraph 99:

I would now like to say a special word to *women who have had an abortion*. The Church is aware of the many factors which may have influenced your decision, and she does not doubt that in many cases it was a painful and even shattering decision. The wound in your heart may not yet have healed. Certainly what happened was and remains terribly wrong. But do not give in to discouragement and do not lose hope. Try rather to understand what happened and face it honestly. If you have not already done so, give yourselves over with humility and trust to repentance. The Father of mercies is ready to give you his forgiveness and his peace in the Sacrament of Reconciliation. You will come to understand that nothing is definitively lost and you will also be able to ask forgiveness from your child, who is now living in the Lord. With the friendly and expert help and advice of other people, and as a result of your own painful experience, you can be among the most eloquent defenders of everyone's right to life. Through your commitment to life, whether by accepting the birth of other children or by welcoming and caring for those most in need of someone to be close to them, you will become promoters of a new way of looking at human life.

John Paul II, writing about abortion in *Crossing the Threshold of Hope* (206-207):

> ...we are witnessing true human tragedies. Often *the woman is the victim of male selfishness,* in the sense that the man, who has contributed to the conception of the new life, does not want to be burdened with it and leaves the responsibility to the woman, as if it were "her fault" alone. So, precisely when the woman most needs the man's support, he proves to be a cynical egotist, capable of exploiting her affection or weakness, yet stubbornly resistant to any sense of responsibility for his own action....
>
> ...[I]*n firmly rejecting "pro-choice" it is necessary to become courageously "pro-woman," promoting a choice that is truly in favor of women.* It is precisely the woman, in fact, who pays the highest price, not only for her motherhood, but even more for its destruction, for the suppression of the life of the child who has been conceived. The only honest stance, in these cases, *is that of radical solidarity with the woman.* It is not right to leave her alone. The experiences of many counseling centers show that the woman does not want to suppress the life of the child she carries within her. If she is supported in this attitude, and if at the same time she is freed from the intimidation of those around her, then she is even capable of heroism. As I have said, numerous counseling centers are witness to this....

"Whatever is opposed to life itself, such as any type of murder, genocide, abortion, euthanasia, or willful self-destruction...all these things are infamies indeed. They poison human society, and they do more harm to those who practice them than to those who suffer from the injury" (*Gaudium et Spes*, 27).

There are two major dimensions of post-abortion healing, one is spiritual, the other is communal. One woman who thought she was fully healed after confessing her sin to Jesus later discovered that sharing her experience with other post-aborted women offered another kind of healing: "While it takes the blood of Jesus to deliver us from guilt, it takes the acceptance of others to deliver us from shame."

This spiritual and communal aspect of reconciliation is evident in the earthly ministry of Christ. "During his public life, Jesus not only forgave sins, but also made plain the effect of this forgiveness: he reintegrated forgiven sinners into the community of the People of God from which sin had alienated or even excluded them. A remarkable sign of this is the fact that Jesus receives sinners at his table, a gesture that expresses in an astonishing way both God's forgiveness and the return to the bosom of the People of God" (CCC 1443).

For Catholic women and men, the Sacrament of Reconciliation must be at the heart of the healing process. Guided by Scriptural mandates (Mt. 16:19; John 20:23; 2 Cor. 5:18-20), the priest is "the sign and the instrument of God's merciful love for the sinner. The confessor is not the master of God's forgiveness, but its servant" (CCC 1465-1466). In the process of reconciliation, the priest is uniquely able to act as a representative of both God and community. As an ordained priest, he represents God's mercy, which releases the sinner from guilt. Simultaneously, as a merely human member of the parish, he is also able to represent the support of the community which, together with him, prays for the peace and joy of the sinner and the sinner's release from the bondage of shame. Through this sacrament the sinner is reunited with the entire community of repentant sinners who share Christ's table.

THE GIFT OF HOPE

"Hope is not something we can grab at on our own.... You cannot demand hope of other people; you can only give it to them. When those close to us do not have any hope, the reason may be because we have failed to give them any....[Hope requires] an investment (rather than a withdrawal) of ourselves in the lives and struggles of others.

"Hope is transferred only through human beings; hope comes when we are able to reach each other or it does not come at all. Hope is not outside us; it sings in our bruised hearts when some person reaches out to us at the moment we feel like giving up. The Spirit works through the touch of the person who believes in us enough not to give up on us; this action of another makes the deadened filaments of the soul glow once again; it is through persons who give us their light when we are in darkness that we experience

the power of Resurrection. Hope comes to life at any moment when one man reaches out sincerely to another."
—Eugene Kennedy, *The Joy of Being Human*
(Garden City, NY: Image Books, Doubleday, 1977).

ABORTION AND TEENS

Abortion deeply affects who we are and what we believe. Abortion does not simply turn back the clock of time. It is a profound experience that touches every aspect of a person's emotional and spiritual being. For a young teenage girl who is pregnant, the choice is not simply between having a baby or not having a baby. It is a choice between having a baby or having an abortion—a trauma. It will affect how she sees herself as a person, her sexuality, her maternity, and her familial relations. It will shape her self-image and determine if she views herself as good or bad, generous or selfish, courageous or cowardly. Parents who urge their daughters to choose abortion are doing so with the sincere hope that they are saving their child's future. But what is really happening is that they are *shaping* their child's future, replacing the burdens (and joys) of parenthood with the lasting trauma and pain of abortion. They do not realize the tremendous barrier the abortion will become between their daughter and themselves. They do not realize that the impact of abortion on their daughter's self-esteem is very likely to aggravate hostility and rebellion against them and to drive her to seek escape in alcohol, drugs, promiscuity, replacement pregnancies, or even suicide.

ABORTION AND TEENS, II

Abortion is especially traumatic and life-altering for teenagers because their lives are in a critical stage of emotional and spiritual formation. When a father who has expressed his love and support for his daughter for her lifetime offers to pay for an abortion, or even insists on an abortion, what does this do to her concept of love? When a mother who is the model of maternity for her daughter encourages thoughts of abortion, what does this do for her concept of motherhood? When those who say they love her, including her boyfriend, say they cannot love her unborn child, or even that *she should not love* her unborn child, what are they doing to her view of what love, family, and marriage mean?

TO THOSE WHO ASSISTED OTHERS IN ABORTION

If any of you have ever been involved in encouraging someone else to have an abortion, pray that that person has been touched by God's healing. Pray for forgiveness because you, too, were ignorant, afraid, and perhaps selfish. And then, if it is at all possible, even if it makes you very uncomfortable, go to that person and let her know that if she has ever regretted her abortion, if it has ever caused her any pain, you are sorry that you didn't offer her the encouragement and hope she needed. Offer to be there for her now, or in the future, if ever she needs to talk through what she has experienced. In doing so, you may well open up to her the possibility of being freed from the pain and despair which she has felt it impossible to share with anyone else. Because you know of her abortion, because you have broken the silence with words of apology and hope, the opportunity for sharing and healing will be restored. Do this for love of the person you encouraged to abort. It may be the greatest gift you could ever give her.

ANGER

Anger is a normal reaction to being hurt. We can even experience anger if we are the ones who have hurt ourselves.

Have you ever noticed that when you feel a bit guilty about something, you become more edgy and tend to lash out more at others? This is because guilt can make us angry at ourselves, and sometimes it is very easy to release some of this anger by directing it toward others.

Feelings of unresolved guilt can also make us very uncomfortable in receiving the love of others. Their love can actually remind us of the guilt which we are trying to forget. When this happens, we can sometimes become angry at even the slightest irritation caused by those who love us. Why? Because we don't feel worthy of their love. With our anger, we are pushing away the love of those who remind us of our guilt. We are isolating ourselves because we don't know how to forgive ourselves, or how to ask the forgiveness of others.

In the same vein, those who carry about an unresolved guilt may become obsessively preoccupied with work or play because they need to keep their minds occupied on anything other than their private thoughts. They are afraid to sit back and seriously reflect on their lives because they know they won't feel happy with what they find, and they don't know how they could ever go about fixing it.

Still others who carry about a burden of unresolved guilt may find themselves becoming irritated and cynical about the joyful things happening in other people's lives. Why? Because they resent those who are happy, because on some level they feel that their own unresolved guilt is depriving them of that same joy.

We see, then, that anger and guilt can often become very intertwined and confused. If we are troubled by anger toward ourselves or others, there is a very good chance that this anger is rooted in guilty feelings which we have not yet given over to God.

For example, those who have had abortions can feel a great deal of anger toward themselves. Anger that they allowed themselves to become pregnant. Anger that they allowed themselves to have an abortion. This anger can lead to feelings of self-hatred or may manifest itself in forms of self-destructive behaviors such as substance abuse, promiscuity, recklessness, and suicidal behavior. Some women and men project all of their anger at those who oppose abortion. They want to believe that, if only the anti-abortionists would shut up, they would stop feeling so bad about themselves.

Some of the women who had abortions back when it was illegal describe how they projected all of their anger at the law. They told themselves that their guilt and grief was caused by the laws which forbade abortion. They desperately wanted to believe that if only abortion were made legal, women wouldn't suffer so much emotional pain from having abortions. But they were wrong. Women still experience the same great emotional loss; the only difference is that now there are five to ten times more women suffering this loss every year.

After an abortion, some women focus all of their anger at themselves. As they enter into post-abortion healing, however, these same women may feel tempted to refocus their anger at all of the other people who were involved in their abortion. They may feel anger, or even hatred, toward their male partners, their parents, their abortionists, or even the pro-lifers who failed to be there to stop them. They can feel anger at those who encouraged the abortion, those who did not discourage it enough, and even those whom they were simply too afraid to tell about the pregnancy. They feel lied to, deceived, manipulated, abandoned, victimized, or simply let down by any or all of these people. In many cases, this anger is justified. These other people did fail them. And it is right to recognize this truth. An abortion is seldom the result of the woman's choice alone. Other people are involved, either for being there or *failing* to be there for her.

One woman, Holly Trimble, has written that, for a time, she became obsessed with trying to "assign degrees of guilt. I agonized over questions like the following," she wrote.

> Was it mostly my fault or more the fault of those who urged me to have an abortion? How much was the counselor's and doctor's fault for giving me false information? Was it partly my parents' fault because I didn't feel I could face them with my pregnancy? Am I refusing to accept responsibility if I don't say it was all my fault? And so on. The conflict I felt in trying to assign degrees of blame was terrible.
>
> I finally realized... my degree of guilt really didn't matter any more and neither I, nor anyone else, could judge percentages of blame. My responsibility before God was to acknowledge that what I had done was wrong and ask for His forgiveness [for both myself and everyone else].... While I stopped trying to assign degrees of blame, it was very helpful to look at my situation at the time of my abortion realistically and it paved the way for an experience of self-forgiveness. One afternoon I was praying about my feelings regarding my abortion and I felt a wave of compassion for the 16-year-old girl I had been. I saw her pain and confusion and felt her grief.... I also felt compassion for the woman I was, who had suffered so terribly. I wanted to comfort that girl and that woman, who was myself... instead of accuse and blame her. I wanted her to know that she was now a loving mother and wife, not a terrible person. I found myself crying "I forgive you! I forgive you!" And I was talking to me.
>
> You can pray for self-acceptance as I did. Ask God to help you to stop accusing yourself and to feel compassion and forgiveness towards the woman or girl you were.... Ask Him to help you see

your situation realistically and accurately; not to deny your own responsibility, but to give you some insight as to why you chose abortion. Ask Him to help you see yourself through His eyes and to give you hope that you can grow to be a person who is stable and loving and capable of living a life pleasing to God.[1]

HANGING ONTO GUILT

In describing her process of recovery following her abortion, Holly Trimble writes, "When I was struggling with trying to forgive myself, I realized I was afraid to stop chastising myself. It was as if I thought that was how I could let God know how really sorry I was. I think I was afraid that if I didn't keep punishing myself, God would punish me. But as I learned more about the nature of God's forgiveness, I realized this was irrational thinking—that actually God wanted me to accept his forgiveness and be at peace...'for the sorrow that is according to the will of God produces repentance without regrets, leading to salvation.' 2 Cor. 7:10."[2]

GRIEF[3]

"Grief is a necessary part of coming to terms with a death. Although seemingly unbearable at times, it causes us to grow and gain insights in ways that might not be possible otherwise. No one who has experienced an intense period of grieving will ever be the same again. If a person turns to God in his or her grief, God can use that pain and sorrow to draw that person close to Him and to teach that person His ways. The Bible tells us that God is near to those that grieve. 'The Lord is near to the broken-hearted, and saves those who are crushed in spirit.' Psalm 34:19."

[1] Trimble, *Healing Post-Abortion Trauma: Help for Women Hurt by Abortion* (Stafford, VA: American Life League, 1989), 22–24.

[2] Trimble, 23-24.

[3] Trimble, 25.

OTHERS HAVE GONE BEFORE YOU[4]

"Before I knew other women who had suffered as I did, I thought I was the only woman who had such a serious reaction to abortion. It helped immensely when two friends shared with me that they also had abortions and experienced similar trauma and grief. I felt a relief in talking to other women who knew what I was feeling because they had had the same experience. It was an encouragement to me to see that they had been able to overcome their pain and lead normal lives. The support and understanding women can offer each other is scriptural and, I believe, part of God's plan for restoration after abortion. The Bible talks about the comfort we can give each other in this way: 'Blessed be God . . . the Father of mercies and the God of all comfort; who comforts us in all our afflictions so that we may be able to comfort those who are in any affliction with the comfort with which we ourselves are comforted by God.' 2 Cor. 1:3,4."

ENTRUSTING YOUR CHILD TO GOD[5]

"While it can be very difficult to release your child to God, it is crucial. You can pray for God's help to do so. I came to realize that I didn't want to totally release my child to God because my grief was all of my child I felt I had left. A pastor helped me to see how badly I needed to trust God completely for my baby and had me relinquish him to God verbally in prayer. A few months after this I . . . [heard] a woman representing an adoption agency [who] spoke about how pregnant girls who come to them can choose an adoptive family for their baby. . . . While driving home, I began to fantasize about how I could have done the same thing. . . . I told myself I could have trusted the family with my baby and been at peace about it. But then God spoke to me in my heart, "So, you could trust human parents with your child, but you won't trust Me?" That really showed me how I had to stop fantasizing about the 'what might have beens' and truly trust God. A scripture came to mind: 'Trust the Lord with all your heart, and do not lean on your

---

[4] Trimble, 26.

[5] Trimble, 29–30.

own understanding.' Proverbs 3:5. [After that,] a peace began to grow and I have become more and more able to fully release my child to God."

ALL THINGS CAN BE MADE TO SERVE GOD [6]

"When I was so ill with depression and guilt [after my abortion] I was continually confronted with one particular scripture: 'And we know that God causes all things to work together for good to those who love God, to those who are called according to His purpose.' (Romans 8:28)

"I had a difficult time believing that this could apply to something as destructive and devastating as my abortion. After all, my baby had died and I was completely shattered, unable to function in a normal manner.... [Eventually] God began to patiently show me how this scripture could be fulfilled in my life. First, I began to recognize that the pain I was experiencing had given me insights on suffering, sin, and forgiveness. It also gave me a great desire to live in obedience to God; in fact, my depression was the catalyst for both myself and my husband to come to know the Lord.... [I also came to realize that] my struggles to overcome my emotional pain could lead me into becoming a better person than I ever would have been without the need to struggle.

"I do not want to be misunderstood. I am not thankful I had an abortion. But I am extremely grateful that God has used such a tragedy to bring me to Him and to teach me. I am very grateful that He has used this to ultimately make me into a stronger person, concerned about serving Him instead of just living for myself.

"God has a plan for your life, too. Be patient with yourself. Spend time in prayer and studying God's word. Let God bring healing to you. Each day dedicate yourself to Him and you will see Him work in your life in truly miraculous ways. You will see how even a tragedy such as abortion can be used by God to work for good. 'For I am confident of this very thing, that He who began a good work in you will perfect it until the day of Christ Jesus.' (Philippians 1:6)."

---

[6] Trimble, 37–41.

Self-Justification vs. Justification in Christ

Sin creates a gulf between ourselves and God. This gulf is widened even farther when we deny our guilt or try to defend ourselves with rationalizations. When we engage in such self-defensive excuse-making, what we are really doing is attempting to *justify ourselves*. This is a futile task. What we need is not *self-justification*, but rather *justification through Christ*.

Only Christ can repair the damages of sin. Only He can close the gap between ourselves and God. And when He restores us to His Father, He does not do so by offering excuses on our behalf. Instead, He stretches His arms out upon a cross and freely accepts for us the punishment that we deserve.

This is why excuses are not just futile; they can be fatal. For when we deny our guilt and make excuses for our failings, we are actually rejecting the gift of justification in Christ. We are, in effect, saying, "I don't need forgiveness because I have an excuse. Christ's suffering doesn't need to apply to me, at least in this case, because I don't deserve to be punished. I had good reasons for what I did."

Whether we make such excuses to others or just to ourselves, what we are really trying to do is convince ourselves and others that we are better than we really are. Such attempts at self-justification are good for the ego, but they are bad for the soul. As soon as we begin to make excuses for our sins—or even worse, when we try to argue that our sinful behavior may actually be virtuous behavior for this or that other reason—we have become ensnared in the most deadly of all sins: PRIDE.

The proud do not need the cross of Christ or the forgiveness of God. They have placed their hope on a series of self-justifications: "I am a good person. No one can judge me. I had good reasons for what I did. Under the circumstances, my decision was justified. I feel it was for the best."

I plead with you. Throw aside pride's false justifications. Be courageous and accept the way of Christ, the way of humility. Admit your failings so that you can admit your need for justification in Christ. The salvation of Christ is not totally without cost. There is a price. You have to give up your pride, give up your excuses, give up your self-justification. If you hang onto these, you are like the miser on a sinking ship who in trying to save his treasure ends up destroying himself.

If your treasure is your pride—which means that you are trying to defend your ego by denying your sins or faults—then you love your ego more than God. Cast aside this false treasure! You do not need that cheap coin of excuses and rationalizations. You are the only one who sees any value in them, anyway.

Instead, embrace the one treasure of immeasurable worth: the justification offered by Christ. This justification, purchased by the blood of Christ, is given freely only to those who can say, "I need you Lord, for I have sinned. You alone can save my life." With this simple act of humility, desiring and accepting Christ's sacrifice on your behalf, everything that is truly good will be restored to you.

But there is a price. You cannot have both *self-justification* and *justification in Christ*. If you cling to one, you will lose the other. This is why you must set aside your excuses and rationalizations. You must admit that you need the mercy and forgiveness of God. If you do not hesitate in confessing your sins, Christ will not hesitate to pay for them.

It is so simple, yet so hard. To admit that we are wrong is never easy. But when we do so, we are allowing Christ, His arms outstretched on a cross from here to there, to close the gap which sin has created between ourselves and God. All we have to do is stop trying to justify ourselves. Let Jesus do the work. He will justify us through Himself. All we need to do is admit that we need *Him*.

NO PLACE TO TURN

One great difficulty faced by women and men who are burdened by the weight of a past abortion is that they are afraid to reveal to others the secret grief they feel over a past abortion. They fear the reactions of both those who are pro-choice and those who are pro-life.

On one hand, they are afraid that those who defend abortion will scoff at their need to grieve. After all, if abortion is "no big deal," if what they aborted was not really their child, why should they grieve? Some abortion defenders would even consider such grief to be irrational.

On the other hand, those who have had abortions are afraid that if they share their grief with those who condemn abortion they themselves will be subjected to condemnation. They can just imagine their pro-life friends gaping at them with horrified expressions saying: "How could you ever do such a thing?!" They not only fear losing the respect of their pro-life friends, they also fear that such a rejection will only intensify their feelings of guilt and loss.

What post-aborted women and men really want, and need, is to be understood. They need their grief to be acknowledged and authenticated. They need the opportunity to share their grief with people who will respect their pain—not turn it into a political statement.

If we want to be a community of healers, then, we must not allow our political or philosophical views of abortion to push away those who are suffering from post-abortion grief. Those who are pro-choice must not deny that there is anything to grieve about when a child is lost through abortion. And those who are pro-life must not treat an expression of post-abortion grief like an opportunity to say, "I told you so."

Both sides of this political debate must simply make room for those who need to grieve. This grief is authentic and meaningful. It must be met with compassion. Not with excuses or condemnations. But simply with compassion and understanding, which are the keys to emotional healing.

"LET'S FACE OUR FEARS"[7]

Am I just too busy to get more involved?

Much of what we are called to do for pro-life does not take more *time*. Rather, it takes more *spirit*. It doesn't take any extra time to preach on abortion than to preach on any other topic.

Am I afraid of being confrontational?

Being confrontational is not the same as being uncharitable. Our Lord, who ate with sinners, also confronted them. Love demands confrontation because it cannot rest if the beloved is entangled in evil. Many think of the price of confrontation, but

---

[7] Excerpts from a series of articles by Rev. Frank Pavone published in *Priests for Life* newsletter, volumes 4(1) to 5(2).

forget that there is also a price to be paid for NOT confronting. That price is that evil continues to flourish, relationships become shallow and superficial, and true leadership vanishes because the leader is no longer able to point out the right path, and will eventually lose the respect of those who look to him for guidance.

Am I afraid preaching on abortion will drive away women who have had abortions?

We preach on abortion to SAVE such women, and to protect other women from making the same mistake. A letter we received from a woman who had an abortion urges us NOT to fear speaking out. "I can't help but think that if I heard in church that abortion was wrong...I might have chosen to keep my baby instead of killing my baby." [Some women reporting similar feelings say that they ended up leaving or resenting the Church because their ministers had been silent. Some blame their mistakes, and their grief, on the failure of their clergy to give them solid moral guidance.] ...We can help [women] on the path to healing by proclaiming the truth about abortion and the reality of forgiveness. When we address abortion, it tells her, "We care." Our silence tells her, "We don't care."

Am I afraid of "dividing my parish?"

The fact is, every parish is already "divided" in the sense that you will find people on different sides of the abortion issue. If we never speak of the issue, we may cover over the division for a while, but that is not the same thing as unity. Unity is founded on truth and is fostered by a clear exposition of truth.... The Word itself causes [division]. "I have come for division" (Luke 12:51). It is the division between truth and error, grace and sin, life and death. [Unity can best be fostered by preaching a message of community support for those who need post-abortion healing.]

Am I afraid of political issues?

Does the fact that politicians talk about abortion require us to be silent?... Some clergy will be silent, saying it is a "political issue." Then, some politicians will be silent, saying it is a "religious issue." If abortion is immoral, where do we go to say so?... If being afraid of political issues is the problem, how much more should we fear spiritual ones, in which the powers at war are much more awesome and the stakes much higher! But we are priests. We do not undertake the task on human strength, but in the power and authority of Christ. Hence, we do not let fear deter us.

Am I afraid that I lack the skill to adequately address the topic of abortion?

[If there is a lack of self-confidence] we need to strengthen our confidence by becoming more informed about the issue.... There is sometimes a fear that we will give the issue the wrong emphasis ("coming down too hard," "fostering guilt," "sounding uncaring"). To help counteract this, we can resolve that our speaking on abortion will always include reference to the help available to women in need, as well as the peace and forgiveness Christ offers through His Church.

Am I afraid that abortion is too complex to be addressed in a homily?

If this is our attitude, we can ask, "How is it complex?" Certainly it is psychologically complex. Morally, however, it is quite straightforward.

Do I feel the people already hear and know enough about abortion?

Most people still do not know the extent of abortion... or the harmful physical and psychological after-effects of the procedure on the mother. Many know abortion is evil, but they do not realize HOW evil it is. Moreover, knowledge is not virtue. [We must be especially fervent in exposing the lie that most women are not "affected" by their abortions. This widespread lie leads people to encourage or tolerate abortion. It also compels women to hide their grief over a past abortion because it is now considered to be socially "abnormal" to grieve over an aborted child.]

———————————

Chapter Seven

Testimonies

IT is important to share stories of women who have had abortions with your congregation for two very special reasons. First, they help those who have not had abortions to better understand the pressures which women face and to have a more sincere compassion for those who have had abortions. Second, they help those who have had abortions to see compassion in the eyes of all those around them and to know that they, too, would be accepted with compassion if they were ever to share their stories. This is very important. Those who fear that they would be "stoned" or shunned by their Christian community if "the truth were known" must be encouraged to hope that the opposite is true. They need to hear and see that "if the truth were known," their community would offer them comfort, not condemnation.

Following are some very brief quotes followed by longer testimonies which you may wish to read or reprint in part or in their entirety.

Losing Respect For Oneself — Stacey, age 18

I had always been pro-life. . . . I wanted to have the baby that was created out of love. I wanted to place it for adoption and give it the chance of life. However, the shame was too great. I couldn't handle a nine-month reminder of my sins. I couldn't tell my parents. (I'm supposed to be the good one!) I would have had to quit cheerleading, resign as class leader, lose all the respect others had for me. It was easier to lose respect for myself.[1]

---

[1] Linda Bartlett, *From Heartache to Healing* (St. Louis, MO: Concordia Publishing House, 1992), 29.

THE ONGOING LOSS OF ABORTION — KATHY, AGE 16

What followed [the abortion] were years of turmoil, confusion, emotional death. The boy I thought loved me couldn't handle what had happened to me. The relationship dissolved. So did my belief in love. I felt worthless. I got an apartment as soon as I was of age. I drank too much, did drugs, and entertained any man who would look at me. I was starved for acceptance. I put myself in the most dangerous situations possible. I had a death wish.[2]

THE LIFE-LONG SECRET — MRS. STONE, AGE 95

I did confess my adultery and fornication to my pastor, but I did not tell him about the abortion. I'm just so terribly upset over that sin. Can I be forgiven? I just feel I can't go to my pastor or to anyone else. I've been carrying around this guilt for over 50 years. What a terrible person and sinner I am. Can God ever accept me?[3]

TRYING TO FIND PEACE — AUDREY, AGE 72

I was devastated after a broken engagement in early 1945. The abortion ruined my life, and made me feel completely unworthy. I'm old, tired and in pain. I have to get ready to meet my Maker in *Peace*!

I've prayed, and cried, and felt I had to atone for it all my life. I miss my daughter and need her so much. I'm completely alone. and now say I have a daughter who would be 50 years old if she had lived. I've named her "Angela," my angel, and I pray to her for help.

THE GRANDMOTHER'S PAIN

I find myself full of grief for my grandchild. I've shed many tears for this little one and for our daughter. Nothing will bring

---

[2] Bartlett, 30.
[3] Bartlett, 31.

Testimonies   79

this baby back, and I'm afraid for our daughter when reality sets
in. I am desperate in my need to give her help. I don't want to see
her suffer all her life.[4]

Words from a Father – Anonymous

How ever can I explain it? Tell me, where do I begin,
to try and justify the cause of just another sin?
I remember the day she told me, and the fear within her eyes.
I hid my love for you behind "it's-your-decision" lies.

How could I fight a verdict that she so quickly made?
All I could do was love her, and try to ease her pain.
I guess I always thought that atonement could be mine—
if we had another child someday, we could undo this tragic crime.

I wish that I could blame her, to help relieve my guilt,
But I only blame myself, and I know I always will.
I should have protected you, instead of her or me.
But I loved her so much, living for her touch....
That's what I hope you'll see.

Now, I see you up in heaven, your finger pointing down,
upon the lap of Christ, millions of innocents, gathered 'round.
Knowing you are in heaven, offers some relief to me
because our all-forgiving God has promised to set me free.

I know we'll be joined together, as family once again
when our time on earth is over and our eternity can begin.
So please forgive us both, for such a selfish task.
Just let her know you love her; it's all I'll ever ask.

"Unable To Forgive Myself"– Liane's Story

Following my second abortion, my relationship to the man I was
living with changed dramatically. I contradicted everything he
said, I resented him, my stomach ached every time he touched me.
I was totally numb. I never smiled. I had no idea how to have fun.

---

[4] Bartlett, 35.

The next ten years were difficult and painful—but I never knew why. I just knew something was wrong, and on many occasions, I felt like committing myself to a mental hospital. For years, I had strong desires to cut myself while cooking, and when I did, I passed it off as accidents. I had to fight with myself to control my car because I wanted to crash into the side of the freeway wall. I have three children I've been unable to bond with. I was unable to hug them or tell them I loved them. I turned away from them and showed them no feelings. I did not have the love for myself to know how to love them.

What gave me the most pain was the inability to forgive myself. I had been going to confession for twelve years, confessing the same sin of abortion, but I was unable to grasp the gift of forgiveness. The priests whom I confessed to, through no fault of their own, did not know how to handle the situation. I left the confessional feeling as empty as when I went in. Every few weeks the voices of guilt and shame screamed so loudly I had to go and confess once more.

My search for healing continued.... [I joined Open Arms, a post-abortion healing group.] It was there I began to learn that I was not crazy, that others had experienced the same feelings and behaviors as I did. Finally, I was being understood. When I finished [meeting with] the support group, I had a new outlook on life.... I began to grab at the truth that I was really a child of God. Finally, I accepted God's forgiveness, and I forgave myself.[5]

NOWHERE TO TURN – MARION'S STORY [6]

Marion was raised in a chaotic, abusive family, which resulted in her parents' divorce when she was thirteen. After the divorce, her mother began abusing drugs and alcohol and became promiscuous with men she would pick up at bars. Because she was desperate for affection, Marion deliberately became pregnant at the age of fifteen, hoping to be able to move out and have her own family. When she went for a free pregnancy test at Planned Parenthood,

---

[5] Pat King, *After Abortion: Stories of Healing* (Ligouri, MO: Ligouri Publications, 1992), 10, 19–20.

[6] Adapted from a testimony recounted in Mathewes-Green, *Real Choices* (previously cited), 198-202.

however, the counselor encouraged her to abort. Marion left without saying anything, thinking "I don't want to do this. Abortion is killing." Though she had never been to church, Marion decided to go to a church for help, thinking that even if they yelled at her at least they would help her.

> I picked out a church that was pretty; it had stone and vines and window boxes and I thought, "If God lives, he'd live here." So I went in, sat down in the minister's office, and blurt, blurt, blurt.
>
> Well, he hit the roof. Got up and started like Jimmy Durante, "what's-this-generation-coming-to" kinda thing. Then he sits down, opens the bottom drawer of his desk, and hands me $150 in greenbacks.
>
> I'm fifteen, I don't ask any questions. That would imply that I don't understand and that would be not-adult. So I took the money, put it in my pocket, and he shoves me out the door. I was standing outside the church thinking, "What does he want me to do with this?" Then I realized. [Marion's voice grows very quiet.] God wants me to have an abortion.
>
> I was surprised that this was what God wanted. But it was what every adult I talked to told me was best. I was sad and I couldn't go home right away. So I walked by the river and sat on the bridge. I swung my feet and talked to my baby.
>
> ... I think about that little girl sitting there and I get upset. In my high school... I was the whore, I was the girl they called when the football team wanted to have a party. Nobody told me about God; it was going to take more than $150 given to me in five minutes to solve my problem. I was going to be a problem for a long, long time. And we don't want to deal with people like that. We care about people getting saved, but we don't care that much. Not enough to inconvenience ourselves.
>
> ... So I sat there and swung my feet and told my baby, "I've wanted to have you since I was five years old. I wish I could have you—but I can't. 'Cause there's *crazy* people at my house, and they'll hurt you. ... And I wonder if you're a girl, or a boy, and I'm really sorry—that I have to kill you—but God wants me to."

Needless to say, after her abortion, Marion suffered from extreme guilt, low self-esteem, self-hatred, intense grief, and a downward spiral into drugs and alcohol. To make up for her abortion, she tried to become pregnant again and again. The second time she became pregnant, her mother coerced her into a second abortion. The third time, she miscarried after being beaten by her father. With her fourth pregnancy, she finally convinced the father of the child to marry her, but she was still severely emotionally scarred by her abortions. She continued to be dependent on drugs, and her ability to mother her child was severely distorted by the unresolved grief she was still carrying for the children she had lost. As an example of how the abortions affected her mothering, Marion says, "I got in the habit of just dropping the baby into the crib so he'd cry and need me."

But eventually, Marion and her husband became Christians and found healing, forgiveness, and strength from the only source of true healing, Christ. But Marion's path to recovery was not easy, and it was not just between her and Christ alone. God uses people to touch each other, hug each other, and cry with each other. Today Marion works in a crisis pregnancy center, helping young girls to avoid the same mistakes that she made. From her own personal experience, she knows that she must become personally *involved* in the lives of troubled young women, not because it is *convenient* but because it is *necessary*.

No Parents, No Husband, No Baby— Colleen's Story[7]

I was 18 and dating a man my parents strongly disapproved of. So they "made a deal" with me: they would send me to college if I would break up with him. I agreed, though I never really meant to keep my end of the bargain.

I realized I was pregnant when the smells from chemistry class kept making me sick. A friend convinced me to go to her doctor in town. He diagnosed pregnancy immediately, saying, "Such a shame, another young one." He told me not to worry, that "it" could be "taken care of." He never once said anything about keeping the baby, but gave me a card from the local abortuary.

Although I had no strong religious convictions, the visit to the clinic for my initial "consultation" left me feeling bad. The nurse told me to come back in a week with the money to have it done.

I had heard some things about abortion, and I knew it was probably wrong. So that whole week, I talked with friends and

---

teachers, looking for advice. One female teacher in particular advised me to have it done. She told me that she had had several abortions, that it was "nothing," and that I didn't need this trouble in my life right now.

No one, at any time, told me anything about adoption or keeping the child. In fact, one of my teachers was a nun—and I approached her, too, with my problem. I think now that I really wanted someone to say "No! Don't do it!" But even the nun told me that abortion was the best route for me.

My boyfriend didn't have the money, so my parents volunteered to pay for it. When I broke down in front of them, saying that I thought it was wrong to do this, they told me they would *kick* me out of the house if I didn't have the abortion. My father said he wouldn't have any "little brown babies in his house!" (My boyfriend was Italian/Puerto Rican.) They told me that if I had the baby, I would be completely on my own. I felt like there was absolutely no way I could escape the inevitable.

When the time came, my boyfriend and some friends from school went with me. There were no protesters, no pro-life people. In fact, during the whole time of this crisis, I never heard a word about or from the pro-life side.

I was led to a room with a whole group of girls, just like me, waiting to have their babies killed. No one talked. No one looked at anyone else. They called our names, one by one.

I was very scared, mostly of the pain they said I might feel. With the counselor, I mostly cried. But she just agreed with everyone I had talked to. Yes, this is a bad time to have a child. Yes, you're too young. Yes, having a child costs a lot of money. Yes, it would be so hard for you to raise a child on your own. Yes, this is the best thing to do.

Waiting to have my name called, I tried to convince myself of these things. I just wanted the whole thing to be over with.

Finally they called me in and put me on a table. The dilation was extremely painful. A counselor held my hand and told me not to cry, it would be over soon.

The suction machine was very loud—a horrible noise. They had a picture on the ceiling for you to look at so you wouldn't have to think about what was happening to you. The image of that picture is burned into my memory. They took my baby from me while I looked at people walking in the rain.

My boyfriend got drunk while I was in the clinic. He could hardly drive me home. He was late picking me up, and I stood on the corner in front of the clinic, bleeding and embarrassed until he came.

When we got back to my dorm room, I was crying. I told everyone how awful it was, and how I wished I hadn't done it after all. My boyfriend laughed at me—laughed at me!—and said, "Well, that's what you get for screwing around!" One of the guys from school tried to throw him out, and they got into a fight. It was a horrible scene. I'm sure he got drunk to try and deal with it; he knew, deep down, that it was wrong. He was only trying to blame me for it so the responsibility for it wouldn't weigh on his shoulders.

In the end, the abortion did not "solve all my problems" as everyone had promised. My parents still kicked me out. I had to quit school. I married the boyfriend. It didn't work out. He became an alcoholic and a drug addict. He beat me up and brought other women into our bed.

One night during a drunken spree, he held a knife to my chest. I told him to kill me, that I wanted to die. I had nothing. No parents, no husband, really, no baby, and no self-respect. How *could* he respect me? I had killed our child. How could I look at myself in the mirror every day? I was a murderer. I truly wanted to die. Soon after this, we were separated and divorced.

My abortion was about ten years ago. To me, it's like a bad, bad nightmare, deep in the past, best forgotten. I still haven't told anyone in my present life (my husband, my church friends, anyone I respect) about the abortion. I can't. I know that they would see me differently, and I couldn't stand that.

I've had one child since then, and I'm pregnant again. These children are my joy—and my forgiveness from God. My little boy is so, so precious and wonderful. If I had only known how sweet and wonderful a baby is, I never would have done it— not in two million years.

I now picket the clinics in the area, and I write letters to the paper and give money to pro-life groups. This helps a little—I feel that I need to do *at least* this much.

It's obvious that the abortion wrecked my life. Emotionally, I was a different person before and after it. It left a path of destruction in my life. My family, my first marriage, my image of myself—all a total wreck. Nothing will ever be the same.

I know now the lies I was told, the truths that were withheld from me, the facts that were glossed over or left out. As a pregnant woman, I go to my doctor's office and see pictures of babies in tummies. Month by month, I hear my baby's heartbeat. I'm told how to do everything that's best for my baby's health. Why is it legal across town to *NOT* tell these things?

I am just glad that I'm able to tell others. I'm glad that I can be outside that clinic when no one was there for me. I may not be able to confess my abortion, but I can *fight* abortion!

ABORTION FOLLOWING RAPE – NANCY'S STORY[8]

It was May 19, 1973. I was pregnant from a date rape. I had tried to hide it from my parents, but of course they found out. Then the pressure started. "How are you going to go to college with a baby?" "How are you going to support it?" "It is only a blob of blood. It's not a baby yet." Before I had time to think about what I *wanted*, the abortion was over.

The abortion itself was like a living hell. I thought my guts were being pulled out. It was degrading, and I was terrified. When it was over, something made me ask the doctor, "Was it a boy or a girl?" He answered, "I can't tell. It's in pieces." The counseling consisted of throwing some birth control pills at me.

It's so hard to put into words how the abortion affected me. Looking back and knowing what I know now, I realize that I was going through almost classic Post-Abortion Syndrome. I became a tramp and slept with anyone and everyone. I engaged in unprotected sex, and each month when I wasn't pregnant, I would go into a deep depression. I was rebellious. I wanted my parents to see what I had become. I dropped out of college. I tried suicide, but I didn't have the guts to slit my wrists or blow my brains out. I couldn't get my hands on sleeping pills, so I resorted to over-the-counter sleep aids and booze.

---

[8] *The Post-Abortion Review*, Winter 1994, 2(1): 7–8.

When that failed, I then tried to make relationships work with men, any man. I was driven with a need to have a child and knew if I was married my parents couldn't do anything about it. Then I married in 1975. While my husband and I are still together, we have had to work extra hard because I married him for all the wrong reasons.

Five months after we were married, my first child was born. I was in heaven. I doted on that baby. In three months, I was pregnant again. But this time, we lost our baby at six months. Then the depression that I had conquered came back full force. I can remember thinking, "I deserve this pain. I killed a baby and now God has taken one from me. I deserve it." The doctor felt that I had a weak cervix, a common aftereffect of abortion, and that the weight of the baby was too much for it and she just fell out. Four months later I was pregnant again.

It is hard to explain this need to keep having babies, but I did. From 1976, with the birth of my first living child, to 1985 at the birth of my fourth and final living child, I was pregnant a total of eight times. With the birth of my last child, the doctor didn't leave me any choice but to quit having children if I wanted to live to see the ones I had grow up.

In trying to deal with the abortion, I had to face what I had done and beg forgiveness from my God. The hardest thing of all is trying to forgive myself. It is a daily struggle to accept the forgiveness I know the Lord has given me. And I will never forget it. Only now, I don't want to forget it, because it keeps me from getting complacent. I know if it helps others, I can talk about it. It always makes me cry, but if it saves just one mom and baby the pain, it's worth it.

I joined our local Right to Life and crisis pregnancy center. I have also had to forgive my parents. I can still remember when I walked into my Mom's house and threw down a picture of an aborted fetus and snarled, "See what you made me do?" She has since become pro-life herself and has told me how sorry she is. I still have to fight against my anger at my Dad, because he still won't admit the abortion was wrong, at least for me.

Do all these things help? That's a hard one. Sometimes it does and sometimes the depression is too strong and time has to pass. Not a day goes by that the abortion doesn't cross my mind. It is a constant struggle trying to overcome my guilt and depression, even knowing I have been forgiven. I dread the day when I have to come face-to-face with my little child and explain to her why mamma took her life. But I also think I am a softer, more caring person than I might have been. If not for the abortion, I might have turned out "pro-choice."

TRYING TO SURVIVE — JUDITH'S STORY [9]

When I became pregnant for the fifth time in seven years, my doctor asked me if I really thought I should "continue the pregnancy."

Abortion had never occurred to me until he suggested it. I'm a former foster child. Conceived illegitimately, my father was forced to marry my mother because of me. My childhood was brutal. I was abandoned by my father when I was two-and-a-half. Then, when he reappeared in my life again at the age of eight, it became worse. I survived incest, starvation, and beatings. I clung to life. But the two abortions I had nearly destroyed me.

My husband said, "It's your decision. Do what you want," and left for work. Naively, I began looking for women who had had abortions. I wanted to know what to expect. But I couldn't find anyone who would admit to having had one. I asked my doctor and he said, "It only takes a few minutes and it's over."

Having already had four babies, I am now appalled at how ignorant I was about fetal development. My doctor said the baby, at six-and-a-half weeks, was "just a blob," and I believed him. I had my first abortion in another state. Afterwards, before I even got home, I began to cry. It didn't help.

I continued to cry after I got home. I cried on my knees beside my bed. When finally I stopped crying on the outside, I kept crying on the inside. I felt so dirty and alone.

Something deep inside of me froze, I think. I dreamed a lot about snow and ice, as well as about babies. I felt cheated, betrayed, and manipulated. I went to counseling and the psychologist said, "Forgive yourself," and "Let yourself go on." She didn't say how.

Two years later, I was pregnant again—on purpose. But still, I wanted to die, or at least go crazy so I could escape the torment,

---

[9] *The Post-Abortion Review*, Summer 1993, 1(2): 2,8.

the nightmares about babies, the self-disgust, and the degradation I felt. This time, I waited until the baby was 12 weeks along before I murdered him. My doctor tied my tubes at the same time, and he said he would never do another abortion. I made him tell me about the baby, just as I had made the man who did the first abortion. (The first one was a girl. She died January 15th. The second was a boy, March 29th. I learned to dread every January and March.)

I wasn't told that there could be complications which wouldn't be discovered for years. I wasn't told that the strength of the suction machine is such that it can turn a uterus nearly completely inside out. I had to have an early hysterectomy because of it.

I wasn't told that having an abortion would lead to unbelievable self-hatred that would consume me and lead to distrust, suspicion, and the utter inability to care about myself or others—including my four children. I wasn't told that hearing babies cry would trigger such anger that I wouldn't be able to be around babies at all.

I wasn't told that it would become impossible to look at my own eyes in a mirror. Or that my confidence would be so shaken that I would become unable to make important life decisions. My *self*-hatred kept me from pursuing my goal of becoming a registered nurse. I didn't think I deserved success.

I wasn't told that I would come to hate all those who advised me to have my abortions, because they were my accomplices in the murders of my babies. I wasn't told that having an abortion with my husband's consent would end up causing me to *hate* the father of my children, or that I would be unable to sustain ANY satisfying, lasting, fulfilling relationships.

I wasn't told that I could become suicidal in the fall of every year, when both of my babies should have been born. I wasn't told that on the birthdays of my living children, I would remember the two for whom I would never make a birthday cake, or that on Mother's Day I would remember the two who would never send me a card, or that every Christmas I would remember the two for whom there would be no presents.

My abortions were supposed to be a "quick-fix" for my problems, but they didn't tell me there is no "quick-fix" for regrets.

I had gone to my pastor before both abortions. He said the babies were "just blobs" too, so when I went afterwards and asked why I felt so dirty, he said, "God forgives." I asked God to forgive me, and my pastor said He did. But I didn't *feel* forgiven. I still felt unclean and undeserving.

I went to a psychiatric hospital and they gave me shock treatments. It didn't help.

The nightmares continued. I became a workaholic. Work didn't help. I became a compulsive eater. Food didn't help. I became an anorexic as a form of self-punishment. That came close to killing me; I had two strokes.

I tried alcohol. It only helped temporarily. The torment would still be there when I woke up. That effort to escape the pain only lasted two months.

A friend of mine told me she was considering an abortion. I tried to talk her out of it. But I failed.

I worked at a crisis pregnancy center for a year. But that didn't help—three clients aborted. I started the only pro-life organization in southeast Kansas, and was president for a year, and that didn't help.

I honestly believe that the only thing that is going to help, is to find out that someone decided against abortion because God worked in them through my story. Maybe I'm wrong, though.

One thing I have learned—God's forgiveness doesn't depend on whether I "feel" forgiven. And it certainly doesn't depend on whether I *deserve* forgiveness. It is based on His Grace, and that awes me! Regardless of what my head says, God's Word says in 1 John 1:9 that if I confess my sins, He *will* forgive me. I have, and He does not lie.

THE DREAM – KATHY'S STORY [10]

The abortion clinic encouraged the use of a general anesthesia, which only added a little more to the cost. Kathy agreed, happy to accept anything which would make it easier to get through the day. Like so many others, she didn't want to have an abortion. But in her situation, it was the right thing to do—the only thing she could do. It upset her just to think about it, so she was trying not to, and she welcomed the anesthesia. It worked quickly, and she began to dream:

---

[10] *The Post-Abortion Review*, Spring 1995, 3(2): 8.

I dreamed that I was contentedly floating in a beautiful pool, enjoying the clear sky. It was very peaceful. But then I noticed that my legs were becoming entangled in the hose of one of those vacuums they use to clean a pool. At first I was just annoyed to have my peaceful swim disturbed. Then the pain struck. I was trapped by the suction of the hose. It began pulling me apart, piece by piece. I cried and pleaded for someone to stop it, but there was no stopping it. Piece by piece, I watched-myself being pulled apart, thinking how unfair it was that I was being denied the joy I had known only a few minutes before. When it was over, I was just aware of floating through the darkness of the tube, and then there was a sharp slapping on my thigh and a rude voice shouting, "Get up." The nurse at the abortion clinic was waking me. The dream was over, but I couldn't get it out of my mind.

Kathy did not need a psychiatrist or soothsayer to explain to her the significance of her dream. She simply "stuffed it in a box" marked "DO NOT OPEN," along with all her other feelings about her abortion, and hid it away. Guilt and grief occasionally surfaced, but she generally coped well for many years. But eventually, after marriage and the birth of her second child, she increasingly felt the need to confront her hidden secret. She was drawn to greater involvement in her church and finally found forgiveness in confessing her sin to God and submitting herself to the Judgeship of Christ.

What happened to my box? The old box was now destroyed; God removed my sins from me as far as the east is from the west. But the memories remained; a mother does not easily forget her children. So I gathered its contents up and put them into a new box—one that was covered by the blood of the Lamb and stamped "FORGIVEN" on every side. I was set free from the guilt and condemnation of my sin; I knew I could now stand before God because I had received His pardon. But standing before man was another matter.

Kathy continued to hide her greatest secret. Even though she had been forgiven by God, it was so shameful a secret that she could not endure the thought of her friends or family knowing what she had done. But many years later, 19 years after her abortion, on Christmas eve of 1992, Kathy's feelings of grief were stirring and she prayed to God:

"Why did you give me that dream? Why did you give it to me when it was too late to save my baby?" His simple and profound reply was, "I didn't give it to you to save your baby; I gave it to you to save other babies." It was then that I realized that through my dream, God, in His sovereign and merciful way, had allowed *me* to taste the *reality*, the *torment*, the *pain*, and the *injustice* of my child's death.

I contacted the local crisis pregnancy center, thinking that this could be the arena God may use in which my dream and testimony could "save the lives of other babies." I was interested in training as a counselor, but they were interested in my first attending their post-abortion support group. I thought, "The Lord has forgiven me; my guilt is gone." But I had yet to learn that while it takes the blood of Jesus to deliver us from guilt, it takes the acceptance of others to deliver us from shame.

God knew that I needed this small, intimate group, made up of abortion victims like myself. I could be confident in their acceptance of me. Through this sharing with others like myself, I began my journey to be free of my shame.

CHAPTER EIGHT

A CHECKLIST OF ACTION STEPS

1. Give a series of sermons on compassion, grief, and forgiveness, such as outlined herein. Review these points at least twice a year for the benefit of new members of the congregation and for the old members who didn't quite believe it all the first time.

2. Keep an audio or video tape of your sermons on post-abortion healing and forgiveness in your church office. Periodically publish a notice that the tapes are available for loan to anyone who has had an abortion or knows of someone who needs to hear a message of God's mercy and forgiveness for those who have been involved in abortion. These frequent reminders reach out to new members and remind the general congregation that your church is a haven of support and healing for those who have been scarred by abortion.

3. Publish pro-woman/pro-life "blurbs" in your weekly bulletin. You may wish to pick a paragraph or two from this book or other books on post-abortion healing, or compose your own words of encouragement. Or create a four- to six-week bulletin insert program similar to the "Healing the Wounds" inserts described in the list of "Resources," which is the last section of this book.

4. Publish a poem from a woman who has been reconciled after her abortion. These can be readily found in *The Post-Abortion Review* and in many of the books on post-abortion healing listed under "Resources."

5. Regularly ask for volunteers to lead and participate in peer groups for post-abortion healing. Allow volunteers the option of having their names omitted from any public notice by handling all requests for help through the church office.

6. Place literature on post-abortion trauma and post-abortion healing in your church bookracks and church library.

7. Start a small prayer chain within your congregation of women and men who agree together to pray each day for the healing of those who have been involved in abortion.

8. Hold a special county-wide prayer service for mothers and fathers who have lost infants through abortion, miscarriage, or stillbirth. Pray also for the grandparents and siblings of aborted children.

9. Organize an interdenominational outreach effort to victims of post-abortion trauma. Develop a public relations plan to attract media attention to this "novel" outreach effort and emphasize the compassion with which the Christian community receives those who have had abortions. Remember, in approaching the media, to point out that as many as one in five women have had an abortion, so this ministry is of great importance to every community.

10. Encourage your congregation, either as a church body or as individuals, to give financial support to post-abortion ministries.

11. Where Life-Chains are held, encourage the use of the sign "Abortion Hurts Women."

12. Invite speakers from post-abortion ministries to address your congregation during your regular service or during a special event.

13. If you have difficulty finding a woman who can give her testimony, have a woman from your church read one of the testimonies aloud from this book or another book. It should be made clear, of course, that she is reading another woman's testimony. It should be noted that it is much more effective to have a third party's testimony read by a woman rather than a man, especially if she is a good reader who can bring the proper emotion to the testimony.

14. Encourage all of your people who know someone who has had an abortion to invite their friends to attend an introductory meeting at your church's or community's post-abortion healing

ministry. The friend who makes the invitation should offer to go along for support. This approach is especially effective if the abortion is an open issue between the friends.

15. Explain to your congregation how everyone can become a "stealth healer." Teach them the following simple, non-confrontational, three-step method for drawing friends and loved ones into post-abortion healing. This technique is especially effective if the post-aborted person is keeping the abortion secret and does not know that the "healer" knows or suspects that he or she has been involved in an abortion. To teach this method, begin by explaining that the goal of a stealth healer is not to help complete the healing process, but simply to open the door to healing.

    In a simple, conversational way, the "healer" covers the following three points: (1) he announces that he has come to a new understanding of the abortion issue, including why people choose abortion and how it affects them; (2) he expresses compassion for post-aborted women and men, realizing that they must constantly face the fear that others may be judging and condemning them; and (3) he describes how he has heard of a brand new program in the church or community which helps to free women and men from the burdens of secrecy and shame associated with past abortions.

    These three steps are enough to open the door. Anyone can learn them; anyone can implement them. For review, the steps can be simply summarized as (1) announcing your new understanding, (2) expressing your compassion, and (3) mentioning that you have heard of new programs of outreach and healing.

    It is *not* necessary to solicit an admission of a past abortion. Doing so will probably be seen as unwanted prying and will be counterproductive. It is enough to simply cover these three points during the course of a casual conversation. A conversational opener may be as simple as saying, "I heard a really interesting speaker at church who gave me a whole new understanding. . . ."

16. Add materials on post-abortion healing to your church lending library. Study these yourself, so that *you* will be prepared to help women or men who come to you *before* you refer them to a post-abortion specialist.

17. Organize or encourage distribution of *The Jericho Plan* to other clergy in your city and/or denomination.

18. Donate a supply of books and pamphlets on post-abortion healing to your local public library and your area's high school and college libraries.

19. Encourage fellow clergy with stories of your successes in preaching this type of healing message. Explain to them how this approach has helped to heal divisions over the abortion issue within your congregation.

20. Send your ideas, recommendations, and success stories to us. We want to help spread your findings to other clergy in a future update of *The Jericho Plan*, or perhaps in a newsletter. Let us know if you want to be on the mailing list for such a newsletter. Write us at Jericho Plan Update, c/o Elliot Institute, PO Box 7348, Springfield, IL 62791-7348.

Resources

The following is a list of additional resources which you may turn to for personal study, and lists of organizations to whom you may refer women and men for counseling or additional information. Inclusion on this list does not constitute an endorsement.

This list will be periodically updated. If you, your ministry, or your congregation develop materials which may be of help to others, please let us know.

To request an updated copy of this list, please send a self-addressed stamped envelope to the Elliot Institute, P.O. Box 7348, Springfield, IL 62791-7348.

Pro-Life Clergy Groups and Clergy-Specific Resources

American Life League, Inc., P.O. Box 1350, Stafford, VA 22555, (540) 659-4171. Offers free camera-ready copy of *Pro-Life Bulletin*, a monthly insert for church bulletins.

Christian Life Commission of the Southern Baptist Convention, 505 Second Street, N.E., Washington, D.C. 20002-4916, (202) 547-8105.

Focus on the Family, Pastoral Ministries, 8605 Explorer Drive, Colorado Springs, CO 80920, (719) 531-3363. Broad range of pastoral support services, led by H. B. London, Jr.

"Healing the Wounds," c/o Pro-Life Activities Office, 521 S. 14th Street, Suite 203, Lincoln, NE 68508, (402) 477-7517. This is a good bulletin insert program called "Healing the Wounds." In six brief flyers, congregations are educated on how abortion hurts women and how church communities can provide a healing environment for their members. You may find room for improvement, but this set is an excellent first start which demonstrates the power of the bulletin as a vehicle for "soft-sell" healing. These flyers are specifically written for a Catholic audience, but could easily be adapted for other denominations.

National Clergy Council, 601 Pennsylvania Ave., N.W., Suite 900, Washington, DC 20004, (703) 361-2086.

National Pro-Life Religious Council (NPRC), c/o National Association of Evangelicals, 1023 15th St. N.W., Washington, DC 20005, (202) 789-1011.

Priests for Life, P.O. Box 141172, Staten Island, NY 10314, (914) 937-8243.

Post-Abortion Counseling and Training

Abanon, c/o LeDona Leitz, 5060 Horseshow Bend, Colorado Springs, CO 80917, (719) 570-9628. A Judeo-Christian 12 step program which parallels the Alcoholics Anonymous model.

Abortion Recovery Canada, Box 61563, Brookswood PO, Langley, BC V3A 8C8, Canada, (604) 534-4341.

CARE NET, 109 Carpenter Drive, Suite 100, Sterling, VA 20164, (703) 478-5661. Noted for its widely used "PACE – Women in Ramah" program.

Conquerors, 1515 E. 66th St., Minneapolis, MN 55423, (612) 866-7643. 24 hour hot line: (612) 866-7715.

Fathers & Brothers, 350 Broadway, Suite 40, Boulder, CO 80303, (303) 494-3282. Post-abortion ministry for men.

Healing Hearts Ministry, 2717 York Rd., Oak Brook, IL 60521, (708) 990-0909. Grace Kern, Coordinator. A post-abortion healing ministry sponsored by Lutherans for Life of Illinois.

Heartbeat Intl., 7870 Olentangy River Road, Columbus, OH 43235-1319, (614) 885-7577. Materials and training.

H.E.A.R.T., Inc., P.O. Box 54783, Cincinnati, OH 45254-0783. Post-abortion hotline: (513) 528-6040. Hot-line. Developing book, "How to Begin a Post-Abortion Recovery Outreach."

Institute for Pregnancy Loss, 111 Bow Street, Portsmouth, NH 03801-3819, (603) 431-1904. (See also Research and Education).

IPLCARR, P.O. Box 27103, Colwood Corners, Victoria, B.C. V9B 5S4 Canada, (604) 391-1840. (See also Research and Education).

Knowing Heart Ministries, 5705 Quivira St, Shawnee, KS 66203. Traveling speaker: Nancyjo Mann. Specializes in ministry to women who aborted in second or third trimester.

Last Harvest Ministries, P.O. Box 462192, Garland, TX 75046, (800)-422-4542 or 888-HOPE-4-ME. Support materials and training.

National Office of Post-Abortion Reconciliation and Healing, P.O. Box 07477, Milwaukee, WI 53207-0477, (414) 483-4141 and 800-5WE-CARE. National referral network and training in post-abortion counseling. Coordinates Project Rachel programs in Catholic dioceses.

MARC Ministries, c/o Wayne Brauning, 237 S. 13th Ave., Coatsville, PA 19320, (610) 384-3210. Post-abortion recovery for men. Support materials and counseling.

Open Arms, P.O. Box 9292, Colorado Springs, CO 80932, (719) 573-5790. Support materials and training.

Post-Abortion Ministries, P.O. Box 281463, Memphis, TN 38168-1463, (901) 837-3343. Support materials and training.

Project Rachel. (See National Office of Post-Abortion Reconciliation and Healing.)

Victims of Choice, P.O. Box 815, Naperville, IL 60566-0815, (708) 378-1680. Support materials and training.

Post-Abortion Research and Education

American Victims of Abortion, c/o NRLC, 419-7th St., N.W., Suite 500, Washington, DC 20004, (202) 626-8800. Public education and advocacy.

Association for Interdisciplinary Research in Values and Social Change, c/o NRLC, 419-7th St., N.W., Suite 500, Washington, DC 20004, (202) 626-8800. Publishes *Research Bulletin*, a scholarly review of research on post-abortion issues, six times per year.

Elliot Institute, P.O. Box 7348, Springfield, IL 62791, (217) 546-9522. Publishes *The Post-Abortion Review*, brochures, and book length

materials under the imprint Acorn Books. Also undertakes original research projects. To assist you in your ongoing ministry to
the women and men who have been involved in abortion, we
encourage you to subscribe to *The Post-Abortion Review*, which is
a quarterly publication of the Elliot Institute and is edited by this
book's author. The recommended donation to receive *The Post-
Abortion Review* is $20, though we would be glad to send it to you
for a smaller donation if that is all you can afford.

Institute for Pregnancy Loss, 111 Bow Street, Portsmouth, NH
03801-3819, (603) 431-1904. Publishes research monographs. Does
original research. Therapy.

IPLCARR, P.O. Box 27103, Colwood Corners, Victoria, B.C. V9B 5S4
Canada, (604) 391-1840. Original research. Therapy. Some materials
on counseling strategies.

Books, Study Guides, and Pamphlets

Loraine Allison, *Finding Peace After Abortion* (St. Meinrad, IN:
Abbey Press, 1990).

Linda Allison-Lewis, *When Someone You Know Has Had an Abortion*
(Ligouri, MO: Ligouri Publications, 1992).

Linda Bartlett, *From Heartache to Healing: Coping with the Effects of
Abortion* (St. Louis, MO: Concordia Publishing House, 1992).

Theresa Karminski Burke with Barbara Cullen, *Rachel's Vineyard:
A Psychological and Spiritual Journey of Post-Abortion Healing*
(New York: Alba House, 1995).

Linda Cochrane, *Women in Ramah: A Post-Abortion Bible Study*
(Falls Church, VA: Christian Action Council, 1987).

Linda Cochrane and Susan Ficht, *A Time to Heal* (Route 164 Box
232, Patterson, NY: Valley Publishing, 1994).

Douglas Crawford and Michael Mannion, *Psycho-Spiritual Healing
After Abortion* (Kansas City, MO: Sheed & Ward, 1987).

John Dillon, *A Path to Hope: For Parents of Aborted Children and
Those Who Minister to Them* (Mineola, NY: Resurrection Press,
1990).

Peter Doherty, ed., *Post-Abortion Syndrome: Its Wide Ramifications* (Portland, OR: International Specialized Books Services, Inc. and Four Courts Press, 1995).

Sheila Fabricant, Matthew Linn, and Dennis Linn, *Healing Relationships with Miscarried, Aborted and Stillborn Babies* (Kansas City, MO: Sheed & Ward, 1985).

Holly Francis, *5 Steps Toward Post-Abortion Healing* (Boston, MA: St. Paul Books & Media, 1992).

Luci Freed and Penny Yvonne Salazar, *A Season to Heal: Help and Hope for Those Working Through Post-Abortion Stress* (Nashville, TN: Thomas Nelson Publishers, 1993).

Debra Jones, *Rainbows in the Night: Bible Study for Individuals or Groups* (Memphis, TN: Post-Abortion Ministries).

Nola Jones, *Post-Abortion Syndrome: A Therapy Model for Crisis Intervention* (Naperville, IL: Victims of Choice, 1989).

Pat King, *After Abortion: Stories of Healing* (Ligouri, MO: Liguori Publications, 1992).

Pat King, *Catholic Women and Abortion* (Kansas City, MO: Sheed & Ward, 1994).

Pam Koerbel, *A Guide to Effective Post-Abortion Support Groups* (Memphis, TN: Post-Abortion Ministries).

Pam Koerbel, *If I Knew Then: A Collection of Post-Abortion Poems* (Memphis, TN: Post-Abortion Ministries).

David Mall and Walter Watts, eds., *The Psychological Aspects of Abortion* (Washington, DC: University Publications of America, 1979).

Michael Mannion, *Abortion and Healing: A Cry to Be Whole* (Kansas City, MO: Sheed & Ward, 1986).

Michael Mannion, ed., *Post-Abortion Aftermath* (Kansas City, MO: Sheed & Ward, 1994).

Michael Mannion, ed., *Spiritual Reflections of a Pro-Life Pilgrim* (Kansas City, MO: Sheed & Ward, 1994).

Frederica Mathewes-Green, *Real Choices* (Sisters, OR: Multnomah Books, 1994).

Kenneth McCall, *Healing the Family Tree* (London: Sheldon Press, 1982).

Nancy Michels, *Helping Women Recover from Abortion* (Minneapolis, MN: Bethany House Publishers, 1988).

Philip Ney and Marie Peeters, *Hope Alive: Post-Abortion & Abuse Treatment (A Training Manual for Therapists)* (Victoria, British Columbia, 1993).

Philip Ney and Marie Peeters, *How to Talk with Your Children About Your Abortion: A Practical Guide for Parents* (Victoria, British Columbia: Pioneer Publishing, 1993).

Philip Ney and Marie Peeters, *Post-Abortion Survivors Syndrome* (Victoria, British Columbia: Pioneer Publishing, 1993).

David C. Reardon, *Aborted Women, Silent No More* (Chicago: Loyola University Press, 1987).

David C. Reardon, *Making Abortion Rare: A Healing Strategy for a Divided Nation* (Springfield, IL: Acorn Books, 1996).

Teri Reisser and Paul Reisser, *Help for the Post-Abortion Woman* (Grand Rapids, MI: Zondervan Publishing House, 1989).

Terry Selby, *The Mourning After: Help for Post-Abortion Syndrome* (Grand Rapids, MI: Baker Book House, 1990).

Anne Speckhard, *Post-Abortion Counseling: A Manual for Christian Counselors* (Falls Church, VA: Christian Action Council, 1987).

Anne Speckhard, *Psycho-Social Stress Following Abortion* (Kansas City, MO: Sheed & Ward, 1987).

Susan Stanford-Rue, *Will I Cry Tomorrow* (Grand Rapids, MI: Fleming H. Revell, 1990).

Thomas Strahan, *Major Articles and Books Concerning the Detrimental Effects of Abortion* (Charlottesville, VA: The Rutherford Institute, 1993).

Leo Thomas and Jan Alkire, *Healing As A Parish Ministry* (Tacoma, WA: Institute for Christian Ministries, 1994).

Holly Trimble, *Healing Post-Abortion Trauma: Help for Women Hurt by Abortion* (Stafford, VA: American Life League, 1988).

Jeannette Vought, *Post-Abortion Trauma: 9 Steps to Recovery* (Grand Rapids, MI: Zondervan Publishing House, 1991).

Finally, something new to say about abortion.

This innovative three-pronged strategy for political, pastoral, and educational reform is reshaping the American abortion debate.

Making
Abortion
Rare

*A Healing Strategy
for a Divided Nation*
David C. Reardon

"Practical and realistic, yet free of moral compromise...*Making Abortion Rare* will accomplish what its title claims—and much more....Brilliant."
— *Rev. Paul Marx, Founder, Human Life International*

"This is exactly what women who have had abortions have been wanting to hear....I pray that this book will be widely read. It provides us with the road map to a kinder and gentler pro-life movement, one which will achieve far more, far more quickly, than we have ever achieved in the past."
— *Nancyjo Mann, Founder, Women Exploited by Abortion*

"David Reardon has shown a rare grasp of the current dynamics of the abortion controversy as it is today. His analysis and suggested pro-life strategy are right on the mark."
— *J.C. Willke, M.D., Pres., International Right to Life Federation*

"Under the old rules of the abortion debate, where the rights of women and the unborn were in opposition, there was no room for agreement. But Reardon has changed the rules....From this point on, the abortion debate will never be the same."
— *Mark Crutcher, President, Life Dynamics; Author, Lime 5*

Published by Acorn Books   **USA $14.95/CANADA $19.95**
Toll Free Orders: 1 (800) BOOK-LOG   *Quantity discounts available*

Stay informed with
The Post-Abortion Review

"Incredibly powerful! If only more people would read it, abortion would end!"

"I'm so excited about your new publication. I've gone through an abortion myself, just two years ago. This is a much needed area of research."

"Once in a while I read something that really makes me feel great, and this just happened to me. The whole newsletter is terrific. Keep up the great work!"

"Your newsletter is *top-notch*. God bless you for your hard work."

Our readers love *The Post-Abortion Review*, and so will you.

Our quarterly publication focuses on the impact of abortion on women, men, siblings and society. In includes summaries of the latest research findings, first hand testimonies, and critiques of pro-abortion propaganda, and the latest development in post-abortion healing and the pro-woman/pro-life effort.

Here are some titles from the information-packed issues you have already missed:

- Abortion and the Feminization of Poverty
- New Study Confirms Link Between Abortion and Substance Abuse
- Rape, Incest, and Abortion: Searching Beyond the Myths
- Two Senseless Deaths: The Long Road to Recovery

The Post-Abortion Review is published by the Elliot Institute and edited by David Reardon, Ph.D., author of *Aborted Women, Silent No More* which the Conservative Book Club calls "the most powerful book ever published on abortion."

The Post-Abortion Review is available only to financial supporters of the Elliot Institute, a 501(c)3 organization which is entirely dependent on the financial gifts of its supporters. Your tax deductible gift will support our research and education efforts. Together, we can make a difference.

The recommended donation to receive *The Post-Abortion Review* is $20. As a special introductory offer, we will send you *The Post-Abortion Review* for any donation over $15. Donors of $30 or more may request a free copy of *Making Abortion Rare: A Healing Strategy for a Divided Nation* (a $15 value) in addition to four informative issues of *The Post-Abortion Review*.

Send your donation to:
The Post-Abortion Review
P.O. Box 7348-A
Springfield, IL 62791-7348.

Discount Schedule for
The Jericho Plan
Breaking Down the Walls Which Prevent Post-Abortion Healing

Suggested Retail Price: $8.95

No. of copies	Discount	No. of copies	Discount
1 – 2	No discount	1,000 – 1,999	56%
3 – 6	20%	2,000 – 4,999	58%
7 – 49	40%	5,000 – 9,999	60%
50 – 99	45%	10,000 – 24,999	63%
100 – 499	50%	25,000 – 50,000	65%
500 – 1,000	53%	50,000 – 99,999	68%
1,000 – 1,999	56%	100,000 up	70%

Shipping and Handling:
One book–$3.50; two books–$6; Three books or more–actual shipping cost.

Order Fullfillment Center:
STCS, P.O. Box 246, Glassboro, NJ 08028-0246. 1-800-BOOKLOG (266-5564). STCS can process credit cards and checks. Credit for purchase orders must be arranged through Acorn Books, not STCS.

A Note to Organizations and Ministries:
Our goal is to deliver one or more copies of *The Jericho Plan* to every minister in America. To maximize receptiveness (and the probability that our overworked ministers will find the time to read this book) each minister should receive it once from a member of their congregation, once from a well-known leader or bishop of their denomination, and once from a state or local pro-life group or crisis pregnancy ministry.

Excluding postage, the cost of distributing 100 copies to all ministers in a medium sized city or county, would be under $500. We encourage you to use this project as a fundraising vehicle. Excess donations can be used to expand your ministry's resources.

In quantities of 5,000 or more, a special backcover can be printed for an additional charge. This cover would include a statement acknowledging that this book was being distributed through the generosity of your organization or ministry. We can also assist you in arranging for a low cost mass mailing with the insert of any additional flyers which you may wish to provide.

Customized editions which reflect specific denominational or theological perspectives can also be developed to suit your special needs.

Acorn Books is the publishing arm of the Elliot Institute, a 501(c)3 tax exempt organization. Donations for this project, other projects, or general support are tax deductible.

Acorn Books, P.O. Box 7348, Springfield, IL 62791-7348   (217) 546-9522